My Journey to Eden

Lisa Pelt

PublishAmerica
Baltimore

First printing

PublishAmerica has allowed this work to remain exactly as the author intended, verbatim, without editorial input.

eBook 9781630009120
Softcover 9781630009014
PUBLISHED BY PUBLISHAMERICA, LLLP
www.publishamerica.com
Baltimore

Printed in the United States of America

My Journey to Eden

Lisa Pelt

S it down children, and listen for a spell, I'm gonna share a story with you, this story is packed full of memories, some of these memories are from my childhood, some come from remembering stories that my Mama and Daddy shared with me, we spent quiet a lot of time together, doing this chore or that, it seems to add up to a lot of hard work, and more than a few bruised knuckles along the way.

Sons, I want you to remember as much as possible, so that you will understand the kind of people that we came from I want you to understand their hardships, their struggles, their victories, and also their dreams, I want you to add your own memories and I expect this promise from you, so hold onto your hat and your soul, this journey is far from over.

One winter we had no washing machine or dryer, the washing machine was broke, we were broke, and the dryer was burned up, I guess it couldn't have gotten much worse, try adding 10 people living in a small farmhouse, and that means a lotta laundry, we did what we had to, Mama and I washed clothes by hand in a double sink that was outside in a shed, a little more than a lean too actually, Dear God, it was bitter cold, so cold that you could see your breath in front of your face I remember thinking, this was what it must feel like in Alaska or Nova Scotia, where ever those faraway places were. We hand washed those clothes in a double sink and we wrung them out by hand, then we ran back and forth to the clothes line trying to get them hung up before they froze, then we ran inside to the fireplace and thawed our fingers out, so we could run back and do it all over again.

While we were hanging out clothes in the freezing cold, with hands that didn't own a pair of gloves, Mama tried her best to distract me from the bitter cold, so our stories began, just the two of us together, so many times I would ask Mama, just tell me one more time, well many years later She told me over coffee, you are the reason I wrote it all down, you asked me so many times that you made it all come back to life, and it felt good to remember exactly where we had came from and what we had been through, so I wrote it down and I expect you to continue the writings and pass on to your children, I knew right then that this story was already written in the stars, I just needed a way to get it to paper, so here goes , Mama this one is for you

A lot of times we would be blazing through a pea patch at the speed of sound, I wondered why we were working so hard, so early, Mama said" trying to beat the sun child", that pea patch seemed a mile long, and it felt like it went on forever, row after row, that pea patch was from here to asunder, and I assure you it was real, it certainly wasn't a figment of our imagination, it was there in the early morning dew that I learned the most scripture, I had never heard so much" Thank you Lord" or "God have Mercy", this was where I learned the scripture about "don't look back", I learned to put one foot in front of the other, and along the way I thought up stories to amuse myself, all the while my back was breaking and I felt much older than 10, picking peas was hard work, but was always rewarded with a R.C. Cola and a chocolate Moon Pie.

Now it's my turn to tell you all about me, I'm the 6th of 9 children, were we poor, you bet you, did we get commodities and free cheese, you bet you, but we struggled along year after year, and we survived all that was thrown our way.

I remember a house that I lived in when I was a baby, actually I was to find out much later that I was only 18 months old when we lived there, and no pictures existed of the house, but to this day I can close my eyes and see two small wood frame houses connected by a breeze way screened in porch, it was a little more than a shack, on the edge of the swamp how we ended up there I haven't a clue, but according to the older kids we left just about as quick as we arrived. I remember seeing a bunch of beds in one room and in the other room I remember seeing an old white enamel cook stove on top it was a huge blue-speckled enamel cook pot and it was going at a roaring boil, steam was just a rising from the top of it, and a table with flour spread out on it, and a box of salt, I guess Mama had been making dumplings, or perhaps she was simply trying to keep "Body and Soul" together.

When it got dark, that old house on the edge of the swamp was spooky, I can remember seeing one old bare bulb hanging on the breezeway just a burning, and a pile of moths a circling it, you couldn't see your hand in front of your face after dark, we all prayed that light bulb would hold , i t was the only one we had, the bedroom door didn't have a door knob, just a hole , the only way to lock the door was with what is known as a latch, fancy name for a small board with a nail through it, you gave it a twist to keep the door closed. Anyway the youngens were sticking their arms through the hole, and then they would pull their arm back in real fast, and a big black paw would come through the other side, Yep it was a Florida Panther and it's a wonder she didn't get us real good.

Next day at breakfast the youngens asked was that big cat coming back that night, Mama and Daddy circled the house as saw all the panther tracks, well mama just pitched a fit, everything was thrown into a station wagon and a pickup truck with a camper, then we shagged back to town, a lot of belongings were left behind, that wasn't uncommon back in the day, the next family to move in just sorta laid claim to it, sorta like Christmas in July. I was to learn many years later that two graves were found at the edge of the swamp the graves belonged to a woman and a child, I wonder if those two lost Souls are still wandering along that old homestead in search of the promised Land.

We moved to Lynn Haven Florida we lived on Alabama avenue, I was about 2 years old, and I couldn't talk , by the time I was 2 & ½ my Mama and Daddy thought I might be deaf, so they started taking me to every doctor they could find, they were sent to Pensacola , I was seen by a specialist the journey was made in haste, and I was examined by a grey haired physician, he had a stethoscope around his neck, and a flash light on his forehead, he looked me over real good, he listened, poked and prodded, even pulled my tongue out of my mouth, he told my Mama and Daddy that I had all of my pieces and parts and that they worked, he told them that I could probably talk , that they just hadn't heard me, he then took my medical record and wrote on the front, two year old female child diagnosis "Mule Headed" , the journey was repeated except in the opposite direction.

My Daddy told me that several days later , he came home from work, and sat down on the couch, and took off his boots, while he was untying them he could see a bed room door cracked open, and he could hear a small child singing, he told me that his heart was pounding in his chest, and that he tip-toed ever so softly down the hall on sock feet and squeezed thru the door, I spun around and immediately quit singing, he then said " sing sissy sing", and I did, later I walked into the kitchen and pointed up at the glasses , and my daddy said 'sing sissy sing' and I sang…"I would like a glass of water', many years later I would hear those words for one last time, and I want you to know that I sang my heart out that night .

It wasn't much later that I learned how to ride a bike, well sorta, I trailed behind my big brothers, peddling just as hard as I could, I was in kindergarten, and we were going to be late for school, wouldn't you know it the old geezer down the road, left his front gate wide open right across the sidewalk, my brothers swung around it, but lil old me flew right over the top. Just a hollering and screaming, landed on all 4's everything was skint and bleeding and I was just a crying, and my big brothers came to my rescue, sorta, one picked up the bike, the other one picked me up and plunked me down right on top of that bike and said one word...Peddle...and I did... no wonder I'm as tuff as a lighter knot...Thanks Brothers for watching over me.

I am 5 years old and I'm wearing my black dingo boots, they came from the boys dept. at the feed store, and they are 2 sizes too big, but I don't care I loved them anyway, we had a huge china hutch big black and heavy, 2 pieces to it, in a Childs way of thinking I thought I spied a bag of candy hid on the top shelf, I remember clear as day, climbing up on that hutch and tip toeing just thinking if I reached a little further it would all be mine, guess I reached a little too far, lost my balance, I remember falling backwards and yanking the entire contraption on top of me, Mama and Daddy was in the den with company they told me later it sounded like an avalanche and they ran in the dining room just a screaming Mama said, there I laid buried under the hutch, the only thing sticking out was a pair of black dingo boots and they weren't moving, Daddy told me that Mama screamed, "MY God Jesus she's Dead", they hoisted that shelf off of me, and I sat up and said..."Hey, where you hide that sack of candy "they couldn't stop laughing , they cleaned up the mess, and Daddy nailed that shelf to the wall, and I didn't snatch it down a second time.

Our neighbor had gotten one of those new- fangled washing machines, it had a wringer on top, and she was in the shed in her back yard doing the wash, well me and my friend walked in the shed, her mother said don't touch it I will be right back, she ran into the house, and we immediately started poking our hands up there and yanking them back, each time trying to get closer and closer, well that wringer caught me, and wouldn't let go, I commenced to hollering and putting up a big fuss, by the time her mama made it back to the shed the wringer was passed my elbow, she screamed "Jesus God Almighty", she turned the machine off and opened the wringer and pulled my arm out, she rubbed my arm very briskly and told me to go home, which I did.

As soon as I got home, I showed my Daddy me poor arm, he looked it over very carefully then he got an old bed sheet and ripped it apart, he folded it into a triangle and made me an arm sling, man I thought I was pretty important sitting in my red wagon with my arm in a sling my brothers had to pull me to the jitney jungle, we got to buy candy, Daddy gave us two dollars to spend, in 1963 candy was A penny a piece and we had a heck of a lot of candy to show for our 2 bucks.

I recall an old swing set that we had, kind of rickety I was swinging so high that it tipped over backwards and my brother was standing behind me, the dang old swing set came down and pinned him to the ground by the neck, I couldn't get it off, Thank God, A man was driving by in a pickup truck, anyway he saw the whole thing, he jumped out of his truck, and leaped over that fence, and yanked the swing-set off my brothers neck, I know one thing, our guardian angel worked overtime at our house.

My brothers told me that the principal had an electric paddle, and I was just gullible enough to believe them, darn it somebody stole my recess money from my little purse, and my teacher sent me to the office to report it, as that huge door opened, and I walked into the room all I could think of was that dang old electric paddle, so of course I busted out crying, the secretary gave me a hug and a nickel out of her own purse, when I figured it all out I wanted to beat my brother butts real good giving me such a fright.

My brothers had a clubhouse, and I know what was in it, I caught them all gone and I broke in and had me a real good look around, I saw something that I didn't know what it was, imagine my surprise later the next day when I saw my brother throwing it and it returned to him, yep it was a boomerang, Oh yeah, I told my Mama about the magazines with all the pictures, and they got their butts tore up real good over that one.

Our house was across the road from the rail road tracks, that train blew past every day at 4, me and my brother had caught a couple of fat toads, we tied them to the tracks, and ran back to see them all paper thin, I still don't know why we did it, just mean youngens I guess, but we got our tales tore up real good and we only did that once.

We had a great big old tom cat and I took the scissors to his whiskers, I cut off one side and he got loose and ran away, those whisker never grew back, and he could hardly walk a fence after that.

My entire family gets to pile in that old Buick 57 and go enjoy the movies and an ice cream cone, almost my entire family, you see they forgot me, they didn't miss me till they passed out the ice cream cones and had one extra, anyway I'm not mad at them all I remember about the entire thing was the house being dark, and I couldn't find nobody, but I found that mama dog in the closet with a litter of puppies, I climbed on the side of the blanket, and mama dog licked my tears and I went to sleep, when they came running up in the house just a calling my name, I could hear them shouting Lisa Renee, over and over, they found me asleep in the closet and mama dog was all bristled up I guess she sorta thought I was her baby too…the only thing that makes me mad about that entire episode is the fact that somebody else got to eat my ice cream cone.

We played hard, climbed the old willow tree, and ran through the woods like we were half wild, but when it came to church, we knew better than to misbehave, we had some Shetland ponies and we rode them like there was no tomorrow, I remember we always took good care of our pets.

Whenever I hear the words S&H GREENSTAMPS, I'm reminded of "The green stamp catastrophe" my Mama had made my Daddy promise to take her to the S&H Green stamp store, we had licked those stamps and filled up those books and it was finally time to reap the rewards…well early Saturday morning there we were on our merry way, when they pulled up front, Daddy said "stay put", and into the store they went, the first thing my brother and me did was to haul our butts into the front seat, he was the official driver, I was just along for the ride, he pulled enough knobs and yanked on the steering wheel enough that we started rolling backwards into traffic, headed for the gas pumps across the way, an old man saw the car and he could see 2 youngens in the front seat, he pulled his red truck between us and the pumps, folks were hollering and screaming and chasing the car, two of those folks was our parents, they were so grateful that my Daddy gave the old man $100 bucks, I guess we might of been one of the reasons that law was passed about leaving your youngens in the car, can you believe it we were on the 5'oclock news.

My Granny Andrews was cooking beans in her pressure cooker, her house was behind the church, that pressure cooker blew up, somebody yelled Hit the deck, we all dove under the table and ran out the back door, folks came a running out of church they thought the mill had exploded, nobody was hurt but Yep, we made the news for a second time…the tall ones scrubbed bean juice off the ceiling and walls for ½ a day.

My granny Andrews got shanghaied by a preacher he told her that she didn't put enough in the offering plate and to put more in if she wanted her blessing, she pretty much emptied her wallet and then the next week she was going to get her light shut off she called my daddy and he asked her where the money was he'd given her for the lights and she told him what had happened, my daddy visited the preacher at home and got grannies money back and preached to him on the churches obligation to widow women.

We got some new beds, and our Daddy was always real good to folks, when we got something new, we would pass our older items to others that could use a helping hand, we had an elderly black gentleman that kept our yards, we called him Mr. Leroy, my Daddy called him and asked if he wanted two beds, he said he would be right over, imagine our surprise when he pulled up into the yard, on a wagon being pulled by an old mule, and the mule was wearing a straw hat(with his big ears pulled through a couple of holes) all of us youngens flocked around the mule we scratched his ears, I thought his nose felt like velvet and he was huge compared to our little ponies, Mr. Leroy just laughed at all of the attention "Ole Frank" was getting, after my Daddy and brothers got those beds loaded and tied down, Mr. Leroy thanked us and he headed for home, I can close my eyes right now and see Mr. Leroy smiling from ear to ear , there he went being pulled by the sure-footed Ole Frank (wearing his straw hat) headed down that old red clay road, the sun was sitting like molasses in the sky, I can remember the old clomping sounds of the mules hooves pounding out a beat as he headed for home.

It was Halloween and we all worked real hard on our costumes, first we went to the Halloween carnival at the elementary school, my favorite part was always the cake walk, but they had a spook room, you got to walk into a room and the lights were off, they had a bowl of spaghetti noodles with grapes in it, and they told you it was brains and goat eyes, then we got to go trick-or-treating…my brother fell into a ditch full of water he got soaked all the way to his arm pits, but the good news is we kept the bag of candy dry.

It is almost Christmas, and we had gifts under the tree, Mama told us the church carolers were stopping by and all I know is we all had to have baths and hair brushed and be presentable while these folks yodeled in the front yard, while Mama was passing out hot chocolate to 30 people my little sister was busy in the den, she found her gift and opened that baby doll and ran outside to show everybody, they didn't have the heart to take it from her, so that started out tradition of one gift early.

Our house burns down and we lose everything (well almost everything) we all make it out and my Daddy and brother pulled the TV out of the den, but I realize the next day that we have no house, no furniture, no clothes, and I learn to pray just like all of the others, we move to Bonifay Florida and live in the farmhouse that our granddaddy Carter built in 1910…we have an outhouse, can you believe it ?, well neither could I but it would stay that way for 5 years.

I am in the first grade at Bonifay elem. We are now living in the farm house that my grandfather built with his bare hands and the sweat of his brow, I was to learn of the way that he scratched out a living, and kept the family all together and on the right track, Grandpa was a Circuit preacher, he rode on horseback and he covered several counties, he would preach sermons, marry folks, and say a prayer over the dead, when the Lord called he traveled, some churches didn't have a preacher till he made his way back to them, when he was older he rode a scooter to preach, and the name on the side of it, was The Gospel Messenger (see photo).

I have a speech problem, and my teacher sends me to speech class, it is held every other Friday for one hour and speech class is held in a traveling bus, I can still remember to this day after I would leave speech class, kids would yell…"there goes retard"… While I was leaving the bus but I knew they were wrong, and I have always tried to guard each man's pride, the year passes and I learn to come out of my shell.

Back to the old homestead, I remember sneaking the sears catalogue out of the outhouse, I needed it, you see I was training our black Billy goat and he loved paper, I would tear a sheet out and he would leap through the air to get it, he was addicted to paper like some of my kin was addicted to moonshine, anyway there was a huge barn, and a corral that my daddy built, and I would stand on a flat- bed truck and wave that catalogue like a flag ole Billy would commence to running and leaping through the air, he could sail up and land on top of a fence post, his balance was better than the gals in new York City (the one that did ballet for a living)…next thing I knew old Billy sailed off that fence post and landed right in the middle of Ole Hanks back, Ole hank was our mule and he was an ornery old cuss and a habitual run a way , but he didn't seem to mind that dang old billy goat riding the middle of his back, cause where you saw one, you saw the other, we just laughed, and said we was going to put them in the circus and get rich… we came in from school one day and the two of them were gone, we told Daddy and he said, spread out and find them and I bet there traveling together, we combed the highways and byways looking and shouting for ole hank and Billy, my brother seen an old codger sitting on his front porch and he asked him if he 'd seen our mule, his reply was…"did he have a Billy goat a riding his back" my brother replied… "yes sir" and he said they passed by 20 minutes ago, we trotted down the road, and found them and led them home, I bet that old codger swore off the sauce that day for sure, and I often wonder what he thought about a huge mule with a black billy goat standing in the middle of his back, being led home by a passel of youngens…skeddaling home as quick as possible, the sooner we got those run –aways in the barn the sooner we could get to those cat-head biscuits.

One time we had dinner on the grounds at New Effort, well imagine every one's surprise when a car pulled up and my beautiful Aunt Hedy climbed out, she was wearing a halter top and hot pants and go-go boots, the men folks eyes just about popped outta their heads, and they flocked around like bees to honey, my mama was a quick thinker, she left with aunt and went to the house about a mile up the road, when they got back aunt was wearing one of mamas dresses and the menfolk asked my daddy why mama had done that, and his reply was that was for the wives benefits not the husbands, my aunt to this day is still the most beautiful woman that I have ever seen, when I was a kid, I never understood why I didn't see her on TV, she made the women on TV look ugly.

I am promoted to the 2nd grade, and this year will see me with lots of visits to the principal's office, I got paddled on a regular basics, almost as much as the boys, you see I was in trouble for fighting the boys and I even managed to make a few of them cry, I was no longer a sissy.

I remember the grass on the south side of the house was thick, lush, green and it looked like a green carpet, one day I thought the sunshine was so warm upon my skin, and a gentle breeze was blowing thru the willow tree, and there were a passel of monarch butterflies flitting around, and I was just a little sleepy, so I ran inside and took my pillow off of my bed and ran back to the Southside lawn and laid down gazing up at the beautiful white clouds, I fell asleep, and when I woke up, ole trouble was right beside me, his head on the pillow and he was sawing logs, just like I had been, I like to think that he thought I needed a protector, but I'm almost certain that ole dog just liked pillows.

Third grade rolls around and I learned that a girl in my class was a midget, I remember her beautiful brown eyes, each morning after the bus dropped everyone at school we had to report to the gymnasium, it was downstairs, I remember ropes hanging from the ceiling and we would climb those ropes like little monkeys I walked by and looked at Susan, and I could see tears on her face and in her eyes, I squatted down right in front of her, and looked her in the eyes, and I asked "Why are you crying", and she told me," I'm crying because I'm never going to be big enough to swing on that rope", I looked at the rope and I looked at her, and I said " guess what today you swing". I hoisted her up on my back , she grabbed the rope I said hang on and she did, I pulled the rope between her legs and circled her waist and tied a great big knot in it, I pushed and she squealed, the faster I swung that old rope the higher she went in the air, I had to jump to catch that rope and my old black dingo boots kept making a clomping noise every time they hit the floor, well the bell rang and what happened next was a complete surprise, to both of us, I couldn't get the knot out of the rope, and all of the other kids had skedaddled to class, while I stood there contemplating our current dilemma, the lights were turned off, there we were in the dark quiet gymnasium, just two little lost souls, and it was just me and Susan, and she was trussed up like a "Christmas Goose"…I said I got an ideal, you stay right here, I'll be right back…I knew I had to think fast, I ran into the kitchen and swiped a butcher knife, I then ran all the way back to the gymnasium, I very hurriedly sawed the rope off, caught her and sit her on the ground, I then said get to class, and say you were in the bathroom if they ask…I ran all the way back to the cafeteria and returned the butcher knife, I never got caught, I walked into class very late, my teacher asked where I'd been, my reply was "the bathroom ma'am " with my sweetest smile, she smiled at me and continued teaching class I was really one of her favorites, you see on the first day of school, I ran in and beat all of the others kids out, I grabbed the first seat in front of her desk, black dingo boots just a clomping while I ran to that prized chair…it was all mine, and I would of fought a bobcat to get it… she announced to the class that it showed I was "Studious", I never told her that I grabbed that particular chair because she had a black osculating fan, and it was the only chair that could catch a little breeze, and there was no air conditioning in the entire school , and I was nobodies dummy.

The following week, I get to go to my very first, Mother &,Daughter Tea, and guess what it is being held at Susan's house ,well when mama pulled up and we bailed outta that old rusted up station wagon, I was standing in front of my very first Victorian mansion, and they had a Maid and a Gardner, imagine my surprise when Susan's Mother, hugs my neck and thanks me for being such a "special friend", and she seats my mother right beside her, I imagine that Susan told her about the swing and I was praying right then and there that she had left out the part about the butcher knife, anyway back to the party, I got to drink my very first mint julep out of a crystal cup and had my first cucumber sandwich, when we got home I told my daddy about the tiny sandwich and he told me that they were hors d'oeuvres, I couldn't say the word, much less spell, but I knew exactly what it tasted like.

I am a firm believe that you got to do good, to get good, because in that moment of time that I reached out to another child that was hurting, I was able to brighten her day and give her a smile on her face, and a few laughs, I believe that her mama appreciated what I had done and on behalf of her child, and she wanted to have the tea party to pay us back for our kindness.

Junking is hard dirty work, and I should know Daddy took us junking all over this great land, we have squished about a million beer cans, and put them in burlap bags, I have seen my brothers clean pistons, and I have seen enough copper wire, to run the length of the entire county, about the only good to come outta all of that is the fact, that I'm not too proud to stop at some bodies trash can, if their tossing something that I can use or recycle.

Pulp wooding is just as hard as junking, only difference is your covered with pine sap instead of grease, oh well that lava brand soap don't know the difference and it all washes off in the creek.

I remember the men folks were down a long dusty logging train, and the women folks were taking them lunch, nothing fancy, just big old cat head biscuits and big lima beans and a bottle of hot sauce and mason quart jars with ice tea in them and a couple red tomatoes and sliced Vidalia onion, just a tad to hold them till supper, while the men folks ate lunch, the women stood among the palmettos searching for a lil shade, one sister called the other one a name, and she told daddy they was a cussing her, he said tell me what they said baby, and she said they was calling me Sassafrass, Yep that name stuck... like glue

It is Christmas time, and in one day Mama transforms the house, we had a silver tinsel tree, with a color wheel, the colors were red blue, green ,and orange, and the tree had red balls on it, well there were red paper bells hanging from the ceiling , as the color wheel spun around changing the colors of the room, we watched the little drummer boy on T.V. and I would try to hide my tears as a small child played his drum for a baby king.

The 4th grade rolls around, and I continue on my merry way one adventure after another, we'll going to summer school, and I get talked into cutting class with a group of girls, well we all end up at the 5 & dime, and we all swipe a .50 cent ring, on the way back to school, we pass by a church and the door is standing right open and I started walking up the steps, somebody asked where I was going and I said to the altar, to ask the Lord to forgive me, and funny thing is the whole group followed me up the stairs and did the same thing, all I know is that I didn't want to go to hell that night or any other .

I make it to the 5th grade and when winter rolls around it is very cold, and my Daddy buys me a beautiful coat, it is reversible, leopard print on one side, black on the other, and even to this day it is one of the most beautiful coats I ever owned, I wore that coat for 3 years, until my arms were poking so far out I look like a little monkey in it, I thought I was the cat's meow in that coat.

We had the meanest old sow in the county we named her bloody bones, cause if she caught you that would be your name, I remember my brothers putting some corn mash in a 5 gallon bucket and adding some sugar and water and letting it sit, yep it fermented and they fed it to bloody bones to teach her a lesson, about hogging the trough, let me tell you I'd never seen a drunk sow before, anyway she ran figure 8's all over that pen, she didn't learn any manners, but we sure had a good laugh over that escapade.

Mama took us all to revival, it was freezing cold outside, and that wind was howling like a banshee, I remember Mama won a Bible for having the most in attendance, well after church we made it back to the old farm house, in the freezing rain, it was much too late to build a fire, we had school the next morning and we needed to get to sleep, that old farmhouse had a fireplace for winter and a box fan for summer we were all gathered around the fireplace talking about the revival and I spoke up rather loudly and said it feels like a fire in the fireplace, my back is hot, mama said it was the Holy Spirit, a warming up our Hearts and our backs.

The preacher came to Sunday dinner, mama had threatened us real good if we misbehaved, mama sang in the choir, and daddy was Sunday school superintendent, one of my sisters had been standing on a chair just a plundering on the mantle, and nobody knew that she had knocked some 22 caliber bullets in the fire, just about the time the preacher finished praying and said amen, the lead started flying, daddy screamed hit the deck, and we all dove under the table, the preacher tore his way through a locked screen door, and shagged over to the next county, we didn't see him again that day, anyway being the tough country folks that we are, we all climbed out from under the table and examined the 3 bullet holes in the next room, and we climbed back on those benches and proceeded to eat our fried chicken and biscuits, I asked mama why the preacher left in such a hurry, and she said, child that's the thing about preachers, some are called, some are sent, and some just packed up and went. Then I asked my daddy about the word Aman, you see half of the folks at the table said Aman, and the other half said Amen well I asked my Daddy if Aman and Amen was the same man, he laughed so hard that he spit out his iced tea.

We didn't have a lot of toys, but we played in the yard from daylight to dark, we played 'booger on the log , freeze tag, red rover, baseball' and other games, one of our most favorites was called treasure hunt, you would find a clue and walk the required paces in the right direction and find your next clue you kept at it till you found the hidden treasure, sorta like geo-tracking of today but remember we were doing this 40 years ago, my brother was the one hunting for treasure it took him well over an hour to find it, and imagine his surprise when he had to climb the old tongue-nut tree and retrieve the paper sack, when he jumped down and opened it up the sack, the only thing in it was an old dog turd…we all had a good laugh about that.

We had a coon hound named trouble, he was half white English and half Labrador, he was the best loving and protective dog on the planet, his lifelong mate was peanut, a little female brindle, she was half wild, but she was never very far from trouble, we also had the meanest tom turkey in the county, he would fly across 5 acres to attack you on that old tire swing, we would holler and trouble would show up, he chased off that old tom turkey plenty of times, I once seen those two dogs catch a stray cat, and they stretched him like they was trying to make guitar strings right in front of my eyes.

I was at the clothes line hanging out the wash, and here came that mean old tom turkey, he got me wrapped up in a bed sheet and I couldn't get away from him, I started screaming and my uncle Roy ran out the back door, he was holding a cast iron skillet(because he was fixing to make tomato gravy), all I remember was that skillet flew by like a Frisbee, he nailed ole tom real good, and I guess you know the rest of the story, yep we had thanksgiving dinner in July, none of us could believe how tender that mean old bird was.

One time we planted the butterbeans at night in the full moon, and I heard tell that you could take a switch to a house plant and give it a real good tanning, just to make it grow, and my granny Andrews, she was the one to tell me about a ring-tale tooter, I guess that just means somebody that chases their tale in a great big circle.

Our mailbox was about ½ a mile from the house, but if you shagged straight thru the middle of the woods it was about ¼ mile I got real good at running that trail straight through the woods, I was running to get the mail, and I spied a rattler curled up in the middle of the trail, rattles just a shaking, I was running so dang fast that I couldn't stop , so I screamed and sailed clean over the top of him, that trouble charged out of the brush, and he grabbed that rattler by the neck and shook him to death in about 5 seconds,, that trouble was a mean son of a gun, almost as mean as us youngens.

Mama wanted a blue berry cobbler, anybody knows those wild blueberries are the sweetest, so there we all went out with our empty lard buckets, in search of blue berries, we hit the mother lode, and had enough berries for 10 cobblers, I kept saying let's go home, so along the fence rail we picked towards the house, out buckets were full, our bellies were full we all had tongues the color of blueberries, and our fingers were purple, next thing I know my brother let loose a big yelp, yep he got stung by a bee, right on his eyelid, by the time we made it back to the house, he looked sort of like an alien, I guess our guardian angel worked overtime for sure.

My mama had a cousin that was a school teacher, she was sort of citified, or prissy, she taught at the high school, and she was real good to us, she would always bring patterns and extra material to share with our mama, anyway she got out of the car one day and left the door open, I told her, I wouldn't do that if I was you, and she said why, and I said one word… "goats"…she laughed and walked off towards the house, so I laughed and walked the other direction, about 2 hours later she came to her car, and she let loose a blood-curdling scream, that dang old black goat was asleep in the back seat, goat pills were everywhere, my mama made my brother wake him up and drag him outta the car, and pick up about 100 black goat pills, I often wonder how she made it back to town in that hot car, that old goat stunk so bad it could gag you to be downwind from him on a hot summer day,

My brothers took a couple of us on a snipe hunt, I felt Dumb later but at first I believed them, I had a lantern and a burlap sack and a stick, I want you to know that I was calling those snipes with all of my might ,my brother said the louder you called then, the faster they would run into that burlap bag, I had just about everything that I needed, but I didn't have a dang old snipe, after me and my brother figured out we had been taken good and proper, we jumped the fence and swiped a watermelon and carved the heart out of it and made our way home covered with watermelon juice, that watermelon sure was sweet, eating it at midnight, under a full moon, made it feel like a successful mission, until we heard that old Florida panther scream like a woman, we got to heck out of there, like our britches were lit on fire , I just knew that a panther or spook was fixing to get us real good, the next day at breakfast my daddy announced that the raccoons had been in the watermelon patch, and he didn't know they were smart enough to use a pocketknife...we never breathed a word, and we did that only once.

We went swimming in the creek, we got there by riding the back of a flat -bed truck, we tore a streak across that field, the cows scattered, the water was so cold, the creek was swollen it had rained so much, I was swimming underwater, and I saw a water moccasin coming right for me, his mouth was wide open, he was so close I could see his fangs, the closer he got I swear I could see tonsils, I prayed real hard and dove deeper, that moccasin swam right over my back, and I believe the Holy Spirit kept that mouth open, because by the time he got it closed the water had carried him almost 15 feet away.

Mama and Daddy went dancing, they were celebrating their anniversary, anyway the older ones were in charge and we had strict orders to behave ourselves, well just as soon as they drove out of sight, we got the party started, the girls locked the boys outside, and they immediately broke back in a window got busted, and we were watching a haunted house movie call The Hill House, and we got the daylights scared out of us real good, when my brother pulled the breakers out of the fuse box, needless to say the next day we all got lined up and each one got a lick with the belt.

We always had a tore up junk car sitting in the yard, well I caught my brother sitting in the trunk of one of em, I don't know why I did it, all I remember is I slammed the trunk closed on him, and all we could hear was him yelling...snake...snake... well when they got that trunk opened the snake beat him out of the trunk, and I screamed and run off and left the baby, my little sister was yelling… nake…nake.. And chasing me.

That same junk car was a 4 seater, once we knew that snake had cleared out for good, I imagine he lit out for the next county, well me and my sisters were playing driving school, we all loaded up, I was lead driver, then I yanked my door open and said…"take over sis", the next driver slides under the steering wheel, and everybody changes seat , we repeated this for about 2 hours, funny how a lack of money had no effect on our creativity, we were always thinking up games to entertain ourselves with. Time passes, I am now 12 years old and I get a bra, I hated it, it takes my mama and big sister both to get me strapped into that contraption, I also get promoted to being head chef, my sister got married and moved out, that first batch of biscuits I made ended up going to the dogs, and I believe they broke a tooth on them, but by the end of summer, my daddy said I could make a fair cat-head biscuit.

I am 12 and my grandpa is 93, Grandpa Carter loved me the most of anybody, and I was always real good to him, I would run to get his shaving water, and I always hand-washed his socks, and hung them on the line, I was always rubbing lotion on his hands, I would put his feet in a washtub of warm water and let em soak, then I would ever so gently dry them off and put lotion on them, and then put on a pair of clean socks, he couldn't hear very well, and for some reason the he would sometimes call me "litha"…I didn't care I would always answer…"yes sir"… I would make him a cup of postum to drink, I would walk the yard slowly holding his elbow, we would always stop beside the clematis vine in the back yard, then mosey around the house to the wisteria vine and always end up on the front porch swing , enjoying the sunshine, he told me one day that that he had to go away and I wouldn't see him anymore, I asked him to take me with him, and he said he couldn't , and that I had to stay behind, well in a child's way

I began to understand the word death, and I told him that I would be right back, I ran into the girl's bedroom and grabbed a big chunk of my long blond hair and braided it, I tied it off with a rubber band, then I took the scissors, and cut it off even with my neck, and tied a red ribbon around it, that braid was about 8 inches long and was the color of gold, I then took it to grandpa and asked him to take it on his journey , so he could remember me by it, he sit there for a good long minute staring at it, then he opened his coat and put it into the chest pocket close to his heart, two weeks later we buried grandpa at new effort cemetery, and I asked my mama if he still had the braid, she checked his coat pocket and then she gave that pocket one pat, and she assured me that braid was on its way to glory .

My daddy had a distant cousin that lived in south Florida, she called and he hadn't seen her in close to 15 years, I heard my daddy talking to her and I remember my daddy saying, bring him, he is kin, well imagine our surprise when they arrived and she gets out of the pickup truck and opens the camper door and a black child climbs out, and he is just a grinning, I'm grinning right back, and I told him we were kin, later that day we went to town, and I'm walking beside my cousin on the sidewalk and some men drive by and cuss at us, my cousin tells me to walk in front of him, and I said no and took his hand, my daddy runs out of the store and chase off the men that cussed us, and I asked my daddy why that happened, and he told me that prejudice was a flower and hatred was the seed, and all could say is…but he's family, my daddy then told me that God made us many colors and to God we are all kin.

School is over and we leave the farm Daddy wants to move to south Florida, mama said only for summer vacation, when school starts back she wanted us back in panama city, so we end up in Auburndale and we spend the next 3 months picking grapefruit and oranges, I had never seen a Mexican before, now we were surrounded by hundreds of them, my daddy said they were hard workers, just like us, we made friends with a couple of families, they shared their tamales with us the only thing we had to share was bologna, my daddy had an 8 track player in his truck, and while we picked fruit, he played Marty Robins and Hank Williams, to this day I still love the songs... a white sports coat and a pink carnation, and also kawa-liga.

We move back to Lynn haven Florida, , I graduate from A. Crawford Mosley high school, actually the school is being built so we attend split sessions, bay high students go 7-12 Mosley students go 1-5pm and I loved that schedule, I slept till 11;30 jumped up ate lunch because mama had cooked breakfast 5 hours earlier, ride the bus get home in time for supper, now that was the life, we lived on Delaware avenue and we had the run of 7 acres, my brother gets a motorcycle, and I pitched a fit and got one also, it is just a little Honda 125, but I thought I was hot -snot on that, we made a racetrack in the back 5 acres, we took an old wooden door and propped it on the side of an old tore up dryer, I would hit that ramp going 45 miles per hr. and I swear I could sailed across 3 cars my mama heard the commotion, and she walked up just in time to see my leap to fame, she marched right over there and took the ramp down, quick as she got to the house I marched right over there and put it back up there, I was still Mule-headed, no doubt about it.

Behind our house on Delaware avenue is an old timey grave yard, we use to high tale it across there as a short cut, but when it was the least bit foggy the faster you ran, the wind would moan and howl like a banshee, and I swear to this day it sounded like footsteps just a trailing you, I'd run harder and faster, trying not to scream, I didn't want to wake up ever spook out there, I learned right then and there that I was lily-livered.

The year is 1975, and times are better, my brothers are in the navy, and they are real good about sending money back home, we get lots of really nice school clothes, but I miss my brothers, and I am real good about writing those letters, I try to share with them what is happening on the farm, what kind of vegetables we are growing, I thank them for the nice school clothes, and I always tell them a bible verse that I have learned in church.

The year is 1976, and a young man in my high school is blind, I share several classes with Rufus, but I didn't really know him, we always sat on different sides of the class room, one day I glance across the room and he's not in his seat, so I get up and go to the previous class and there he sat nobody helped him to the next class, so I opened the door, walked right in and tapped his hand, and I told him I was there to help him to class, me and a friend swap off every day, one time she totes the book and I lead him, and next time I tote the books and she led him, considering the fact that were white and he's black, we got cussed at walking down the hall, when I got home from school, I told my daddy about it, and he told me that my heart would tell me the right thing to do, and I replied, I just can't leave him there it is wrong, imagine my surprise the very next day, I was leading Rufus to class and I spied my daddy standing at the end of the hall, he had on a blue jean pants and a blue jean shirt, and a leather vest, and alligator boots and aviator shades, and let me tell you, his shoulders were as broad an axe-handle, he said to me "sissy, you had any problems today, if so I'm here to take care of it, and I ain't afraid to go back to jail", well the boys that cussed me the day before spied my daddy and they shagged out of there like greased lightning, and let me tell you I got no more flak about being neighborly and trying to help another in need.

We moved to Minnesota avenue, and I spend the next 4 years in a two-storied turn of the century captains house, we thought that house was haunted, we never seen anything, but we had an old room under the staircase that was dark and deep and we called it the grandpa room, we named that spook lead-boots, cause he sure was noisy.

My uncle Clarence came to visit, and he asked me to play my guitar, I pick it up and stare playing and singing the old song 'frauline', after I played and sang that song, I saw him wiping tears off of his cheeks, and I asked was it that bad, and he told me that when he was 18 and was sitting on top of a tank in Europe, fighting against hitler, he used to tell his buddies that when he got state- side a beautiful blondes was going to sing frauline to him, he then told me that he had to wait 35 years for that to happen, from that moment on, every time I saw uncle Clarence, I sang to him, but that was no problem, I always loved to play my guitar and sing, any place, anywhere, me and my sisters would get so loud that often times our daddy would say we sounded like a bunch on nanny- goats in pepper patch.

I got married and moved away, in the years to come I am busy raising my two sons, they are my joy, My father gets lung cancer and he is very sick, I would go by daily after work and check on him, my sister would go by every morning on her way to work and check on him, the ones that lived out of town would come on the week-end, he is very sick with a poor prognosis, he lives 6 weeks after his diagnosis, and he loses 54 pounds, one night I'm bathing his feet in a wash tub, and he says sissy go home early tonight, and I said Daddy I'm ok, and he said no I want you to go home and write me a song and come back tomorrow and bring you guitar and sing it for me, and I said "daddy I got no song", and he said two words... "DIG DEEP", so I went home fed my children, climbed in a bathtub, had a glass of wine and prayed for a song, in less than 5 minutes I knew my song was at hand so I jumped out of the tub, wrapped a towel around me and wrote all 3 verses, of daddies song...the next day I took my guitar and when I tried to sing no words came out, I was so choked up, well I heard my Daddy say those words me, the same ones that he had said so many years earlier…"Sing Sissy Sing"…and I want you to know that I sang my heart out, my daddy cried like a baby, tears running off his cheeks, my mama cried like a baby , and so did I, the tears were flowing, but I did it, I made that song happen, we buried daddy 2 weeks later at New Effort, and it would be 6 months before I could pick up that guitar and make music, I felt like my joy had been stolen from .

When we buried my Daddy, my grandmother Andrews was there, she was in a wheel chair, but I want you to know that she stood to her feet and said…"Oh Lord, once again you have taken one of my children before me, and I still praise you Holy name, and I know your grace is sufficient"…She was a wise and Godly woman, and she lived by the good book.

In the years to come my children have been a source of joy for me, but my marriage has not, I finally find the courage to divorce my husband, I decided I have a right to live a life free of abuse, so I divorce and move on with my life

We take a girls only cruise, several sisters and my mother and my sisters mother –in-law, well we had a wonderful time, in Cozumel, when we stepped out of a cab, it was a blonde, and a red-head and a brunette, all you could hear was oh la la Charlie's angels, we laughed and felt like little starlets, our mother is so beautiful at the formal dinner, she is beaming with joy, and she tell us in a whispered tone, who would of ever thought that lil old me would be a world traveler, and get to hob knob with the rich and the famous… me and two of my sisters found the slide at the top of the ship we can't understand why nobody else was sliding down it, we spent 1 hour sliding giggling and laughing and playing like children, we didn't know that the entire time we were on channel 6 and everybody on the cruise ship saw our shenanigans, for the remainder of the cruise every time we got off of an elevator of entered a room we would hear…there goes the girls from the slide…our 5 minute claim to fame acting like youngens and the whole world seeing it on channel 6 over and over and over…

Mama had a grandfather that was a P.O.W. in the civil war, the state sent a marble headstone and placed it at the wrong grave, that sucker was marble and had to weigh 500 pounds ,my mama said I've been trying to get that stone moved for two years and I don't believe I'll ever live to see it moved, I counted off the paces and started taking my belt off, she said what are you doing, and I said moving a headstone, I started rocking that headstone back and forth and my sister Tracey joined in, we finally tipped it enough that we could lay it across that belt on the ground, then we drug it inch by inch for 50 feet, then we stood it up at the right grave, it was July and our faces were red as tomatoes, an old geezer walked up and said what ya'll doing my reply was…"we ain't digging him up"…I was to find out later that day, my mama told everybody and she called me her "Blonde Tornado"…

My uncle Clarence was a wonderful Christian man , so kind and loving, I was always taking him and mama to yard sales, or to town, mama was always the first to the car, uncle was always lollygagging, so by the time he got to the back seat, mama would be fussing just a little, so by the time he loaded up mama would fire off at him and his famous come-back was always …"Well scratch off then"…I would just do the driving and the laughing, we stopped at a huge yard-sale and he wanted to sit in the car, he said he didn't need any of those gee-gaws… I spied him looking at a woman's but I showed my mama, she said "child he isn't blind or dead", well when we got back in the car, I grinned and said Uncle, I seen what you was looking at, and his reply was…"did you see the size of that caboose"…we all had a good laugh, after we lost uncle and I was taking mama to the crematory to pick up his ashes, I told her I didn't know where to put the box, she said sit him in the back where he always rode, so I drove uncle home for one last time, he was laid to rest at new effort.

It is now 2005, I continue to work hard, and live each day as it comes my way, time continues to pass by, my mother has another heart attack, and she needs heart surgery again, I leave work and drive to Dothan, she is intubated and on a balloon pump, the air ambulance is on the way to fly her to the university of Birmingham, I feel that our time together will be soon over, I am standing beside her bed, holding her hand, I speak straight from the heart, I tell her that I know she is scared, and that we are all together, I tell her that I love her, and I am so proud of her, she is such a courageous Christian woman, and I draw strength from her, and she has been an inspiration to us all, we lose mama the next day, I remember saying …"God has taken our angel", now my heart is truly broken in half, my sons are a source of comfort to me, I draw strength from their love.

The year is now 2006, I am nurse of the year at HealthSouth, time truly heals all hurts, my son Joshua is about to be a father, I get to go into the delivery room, when I saw my grandson Colton draw his first breath, my knees buckled and I peed my pants just a little, and I burst out crying, I told my son that I watched him take his first breath and by God's grace he would watch me take my last…it was so very strange, but I'd felt like I had fallen in love for the very first time, he is my joy

The year is now 2007, and I meet a Godly man named John, he comes into the eye center where I work, and I started his iv, 10 months later we are married, he is a wonderful husband ,step-father and poppy, we are surely blessed.

In 2008 my granddaughter Aubrey is born,, finally after all of these years I have a little girl, yes I love to dress her up in pretty dresses and take her to church, my joy is complete, my cup runneth over, I love being a wife, mother, grandmother, continue on reading my writings, I have shared a little of my family history, I wanted to share their struggles, and victories, and then I will share some of my beloved poetry that I have written, if one word that I have composed, has caused you to smile, laugh or simply reflect, then these writings have achieved more than I ever dreamt possible, I have kept these thoughts in my mind for so long and my poems have been in a box, shoved under the bed, it wasn't till I got cancer, that I realized, I needed to share my thoughts, and my written words, maybe after you read all of this you can take a moment in time and realize what it feels like to be me.

THE BIG C

hadn't given much thought in the past of the possibility of me getting cancer, why only last July an insurance salesman tried to sell me a cancer policy, why I practically laughed in his face, little was I to know that by august, I would be in a battle to save my life, after 5 surgeries, 9 weeks of chemo, and 28 radiation treatments, I have come to the conclusion that I may actually beat this dreaded disease, I still need 9 more weeks of chemo, but I remain hopeful for the future, cancer can't defeat me, all it can do to me, is elevate me to heavenly sand, I am a believer, and I know that my Lord is able to deliver me from the darkness into the light, now that my life has been changed I have discovered that the simplest of joy's are now the best, I now enjoy the songs of a song bird, I cut out paper dolls with my grandchildren, as we walk outside, and they place broken sea shells and bird feathers in my hands , these are my treasures , these precious moments, I hope you enjoy my poetry and if you learn anything from me, let it be this…"start living you own life"…when you look in the mirror I want you to believe, that something wonderful is going to happen to you, I want you to believe it, just like I do, I can still hear my daddies voice saying "Dig Deep ' and 'Sing Sissy Sing" and I promise to do both because after all of this time, I am still mule-headed…love to all ……. Lisa Andrews Pelt

W e sure spent a lot of time, drinking coffee, picking peas, shelling butterbeans, picking tomatoes, we put our vegetables up in mason quart jars, and also in the freezer, I remember one day my mama told me to make a salad, I had a head of lettuce in the fridge, I went to the garden, and picked pretty red tomatoes, green onions, red radishes, cucumbers, and I made the most beautiful salad, all of our vegetables had such beautiful colors, while I was mixing my salad, I thought what a masterpiece. Anyway we drank a lot of coffee, but mine always had a lot of milk in it, and daddy said that coffee will make my heels rusty.

Miss Ruth E. Elliott was born in Miami County Indiana, on November 6 1855, she married Mr. John T. Carey in 1875, since she was 18 years of age she had been a minister of the Friends church, preaching in the back creek and in Friends Church at North Grove Indiana, Mrs. Ruth T. Carey had many excellent qualities, her work had a great influence wherever she had gone (see photo)

When I was a child, and learned about our families woman preacher, I sure did feel proud, I didn't have any idea what it meant to be a Quaker, and I remember telling my mama, that I thought we were Florida Crackers, not Florida Quakers, she almost popper her corset straps she laughed so hard. My mama was Mary Chlotelle Carter, and she was born July 2, 1931, she was the baby of the bunch, she had 4 brothers and

3 sisters, her father was John William carter, he was born Oct. 30, 1877, her Mother was Mable Elliott she was born Nov 22, 1890, Grandma and Grandpa were married on Feb. 20,1910

I love to hear the stories of their courtship, of the lives that they shared, I love to hear of the farmland that they built their "House of Dreams" upon, Mable's mother died when she was about one year old, the cousin offered to care for her, her dad said yes, so long as they didn't move away, the baby stayed with them for about 10 years

The Snyder's moved back to Kansas, Mable moved back in with her father, he had already married again, and she had some brothers and sisters, Her Step-mother resented having to care for another's woman's child so she gave her all the bad chores to do, one of the chores was roasting coffee beans, the coffee was bought by the bag full, the beans were dried but not roasted. This job was time consuming and also very hot, you spent a lot to time stooping over a hot fireplace or a wood burning stove, you were there for hours at a time, but she could count on being left alone, in the summer time nobody wanted to stand around a fire when it was well over 100 degrees outside, the fire in the cook stove had to be kept at a constant heat, the beans had to be constantly turned, so they would slow roast and they wouldn't burn, this chore would take several hours, her family lived on a farm that was a homestead grant, Her Dad received the grant on June 3 1896, John bought 40 acres of that land in June 1908, Mable was almost to marriage age and she had her eyes on her step-mothers brother John, he was 13 years older than her, but that didn't matter, she liked him and she thought that he liked her too, she dreamed of the day that john would ask her to be his wife, she went about her work and dreams, no one knew what her dreams were, soon John started building a house, everyone wondered who would share that house with him?

Mable knew she had seen the shy looks that had been coming her way, she was right, when he had the house almost finished he asked her to take a walk with him, her joy was complete, she knew her dreams were coming true, john had bought a wide gold band, he asked her if she would wear it and become his wife, of course she said yes, she wore the band for almost a year as a promise ring, they were married the following February, John and Mable went to live in their new house , it had two rooms, a kitchen/living room with a fireplace, and a bedroom, she cooked in the fireplace, this was not unusual in the early 1900's, they were newlyweds and nothing else mattered.

About a ¼ mile from their house was the turpentine still, the Lindsey's lived in a huge white house, there was a stuffed moose head mounted on the wall of the porch, if anybody ever mentioned the "moose head house" you knew exactly what they were talking about, African Americans workers lived in little white houses on the hill and they worked the still. My Daddy told me about the foreman, everybody called him "ledge", he was a huge man with an arm as big as a tree limb, he had lost his left arm years earlier in a terrible logging accident, and he had a small drum that he carried strapped to his side, and many times after dark my daddy could hear the beat of the old drum, beating out the sounds of life, reminding others to come home and rest, and as he beat out his commands you could see folks trailing through the palmettos and pine trees, on their way to and from the still, they would work daylight to dark, I could tell that my daddy loved these folks and they loved him right back, there was an elderly lady that was always giving my daddy a baked sweet tater and a hunk of cornbread, when she passed away my daddy got his heart broke, he told me many years later that she loved him like a son, and he loved her like a mother, the color of one's skin has very little to do with what is buried in ones' heart.

Turpentine was collected from pine trees, and an opening was made in the tree bark, a cup about 10 inches long and about 4 inches wide was nailed onto the tree to catch the drips, once a week another strip was cut on the tree, so the sticky sap could drain into the cup, this was called a cat face because it looked like cat ears, when the turpentine was hardened on the cat face, it was scrapped off and the cup was emptied and put into a barrel and carried to the still, the raw turpentine was distilled and put into barrels and sealed and sent to paint factories where it could be used.

About 2 miles away was the Louisville & National railroad, otherwise known as the L&N, coal burners powered the locomotive, the black smoke could be seen for miles, they had a rail switch there, and it was called the long pine switch, the train stopped only if another train needed to pass.

Mail was dropped off and picked up there, if the train didn't need to stop the mail was put on a pick up arm, there was a hook in the train to catch the bag, and drop mail, it also dropped off in the reverse order.

John had his own blacksmiths shop on their farm for making and repairing farm equipment, the forge was powered by burning coal, there was always coal falling from the train, so the youngens would pick up coal along the railroad tracks and carry it home for the forge, this was a hot and weary job, but the equipment had to be repaired and maintained.

The land had to be cleared for the fields, this was slow back breaking work, using a two-man cross cut saw, the trees were felled, if they were big enough they were carried to the saw mill and cut into boards, these boards were used to build the house, the boards were put up green, so when they cured there were cracks left, this made the house quiet drafty so batten boards were put over the cracks, this made the house much warmer, John had a team of oxen, and they walked side by side, joined together by a large wooden yoke, people in the country knew better than to be unevenly yoked, we can learn a lot from simple country folks, and perhaps save a heartache along the way.

The main crops were corn and peanuts after the corn dried in the fields it was gathered, loaded on the wagon, and carried to the barn, sometimes the dried corn stalks were tied into bundles and saved for winter fodder, I was to learn later that fodder was feed for the cows and hogs.

The old barn had a loft, corn was stored in the top, and hay was stored in the bottom, John would carry the corn to the mill to have it crushed, and then add some sweet molasses, making sweet feed for the cows.

Rain water was collected in a huge rain barrel, my mama said that once a week they got to wash their hair with that fresh rain water, and it gave them the silkiest hair, and offered a real treat when used, they kept a bucket of water on the cabinet in the kitchen, and they all used the same dipper to drink from.

My mama told me that one of her most favorite places in the world was the top of the hay loft, with a house slam full of people, it was the one quiet place that she knew of, she would sit up there and read, you see a thin crack let the sunshine in and it beamed down just like a flashlight, and if it was raining on that old tin roof you could just about guarantee that her and that old yellow tom cat was getting a nap.

Corn was shucked and shelled and carried to the gristmill to be ground into meal and grits, the trip to the mill was always an outing day, one of Mable' half -sisters ran the mill, this was a good time for them to visit, the millhouse was built over a small stream, there were floodgates under the millhouse to control the water, a dam was built up on both sides so there was quiet a large millpond.

The trees growing around the millpond were cypress and black gum, tannic acid from the black gum trees made the water black, to kids that black water hid all kinds of monsters, you didn't dare get caught close to that millpond epically when it was close to dark thirty, the water below the mill was only about ankle deep so that was where the children played on hot days, they also enjoyed watching the ducks passing along in the water, they were always so graceful.

The corn was measured, and the toll was taken out, this was the pay for the use of the mill. The floodgates were opened and the waterwheel was under the millhouse, so the gates were lifted up , the weight of the water in the millpond forced the water out, thus turning the wheel, that turned the millstone inside., the bottom millstone had groves cut at an angel around it, the top stone was raised or lowered to change the grit of the corn being ground, so there was grits or meal ,all of this process was quiet noisy, there was no gossip told in the millhouse, it was so noisy that you couldn't hardly hear yourself think, much less try to gossip.

They grew peanuts, this was considered a cash crop, when the peanuts were mature they were plowed up, the dirt had to be shaken out of the bunches by hand, this was back-breaking work. Peanut poles were put into the ground, that pole was well over head high with cross pieces nailed just above the ground; Peanuts were stacked on this, making a conical tower so they could dry. Once they were dry, along came the peanut picker, this piece of machinery was loud, dirty and ran by a kerosene motor, it took about 10 men and boys to pick peanuts, two men with mules, and ground slides would bring the stack to the picker. The bunches were put into the hopper, the nuts came out one side to be bagged and tied. The hay came out the back, bailed and tied to be moved and stacked. This was also a very dirty job, some of the peanuts were saved for seed the next year, the rest was carried to the market. The money from the sale bought flour, sugar, and salt for the following year.

Hogs would be put in the field to eat the nuts that were left, by the time the weather was cold, hogs were fat enough to kill and have meat for this year. Early in the morning a fire would be built under a barrel full of water, the hog was killed, scalded and put on a bed of cornhusks to have the hair scrapped off, the hog was then hung up by his back feet and the insides taken out, and then put on a table to be cut up. The fat was taken off and the meat was laid on the pine tops and salted down to lay over -night, the salt would draw out the remaining blood and water. The next day a piece of bear grease (this is a very tough grass) was pulled through one side of each piece of meat and tied into a knot, this was put over poles across the top of the smokehouse. When all the pieces were hung, an oak fire was built in the middle of the dirt floor, the fire was made with green oak wood, this made more smoke than fire, the meat was cured and smoked and it would be good till the next fall. Thick pieces of meat were packed in salt, this preserved the meat and made white side meat, sausage was made and the fat was cut into smaller pieces, there was a lot of fat, it was cooked in the wash pot, after the fat was fried down, there was enough lard to last a year, left over lard was combined with lye and made into soap.

In the early 1900's there was a use for everything, nothing was wasted, and getting it was too hard, liver and lights and spareribs were seasoned with salt and some hot pepper, cooked down into a thick gravy and served with rice and fried cornbread, now that was some "find southern eatin"

Once a week was washday, I recall while mama and I were struggling to get our wash done in the middle of a freezing cold winter day, she would share with me the trials that she had went through during wash days of her childhood. She said they did wash on Mondays, water had to be drawn from the well with a bucket, and carried to the wash pot and tubs, water was put on to boil, the clothes were rinsed out in the hot water and put in a pot to boil, the boiling loosened the dirt, which was then scrubbed out on the wash board. If the clothes were real dirty, they were put on the "battling block" a big oak block about knee high, a wide paddle was used to beat the dirt loose that made it easier on the scrub board to get the clothes clean. The clothes were rinsed two times and hung on the line to dry. Sunday shirts and dresses had to be starched, boiling a small amount of flour in water made the starch. The clothes were dipped in that and hung to dry.

On Monday night the starched clothes were sprinkled with water and rolled in a sheet. Tuesday morning they were just damp enough to iron, ironing was done with flat irons that had to be heated at the fireplace or the stove, two irons were heated while one was being used, the other stayed close to the fire, the irons were heavy and this required a strong arm, if it was wintertime a fire would be going in the fireplace but if it was summertime a fire would be set in the wood burning stove. Ironing was a hard day's work for sure.

The kitchen garden was planted first, and then the fields were prepared for planting. The compost was dug out of the cow pen and loaded onto a wagon and carried to the fields, and put in the rows. The crop was planted, sometimes the corn was planted by hand or perhaps a corn planter was borrowed, the kids got to drop corn into the rows, while daddy covered the rows, the entire family worked hard, it was essential for their survival and it literally meant the difference between having plenty or facing hard times.

They grew sugarcane on the farm, when they harvested the cane, it had to be stripped, topped, and cut down, put on the wagon and hauled to the cane mill, the stalks were fed into the mill and crushed, the juice as caught in a drum and carried to the syrup kettle, then it was cooked down into syrup, this was a slow process, it had to be stirred and skimmed constantly, but the cane syrup was not only used on food, it was used as a sweetener, mama would take a cathead biscuit and cover it with the new syrup, boy that was good eating.

They had large pear trees, the pears were made into preserves, and then they were used in pies and tarts, man that was some fine eating, especially if they happened to have hand cranked ice cream to top it with.

My mama had a tiny pet redbird, she named it "birdie", her brother had taken it away from the cat's mouth, and they built is a small cage, and hand tamed it, it was a very pretty redbird, and they left the cage open, it would fly around inside or outside, and return to the cage, but it always came back when you whistled for it.

When my mama was little, she skipped everywhere she went, sometimes her daddy would say ...do that again, and when she did he told her..."you look just like a cricket"

Once a year Grandpa would take the mule and wagon, and go from Bonifay to Panama city beach, then he would buy barrels of mullet, he would salt them down, the whole trip took about 9 days, he slept on the ground under the wagon, and the old mule was tied to a tree limb, he cooked coffee over a small fire, and ate dried hard tack, and biscuits, when he got home, they cleaned and smoked those mullet, times were hard, families that had nothing or no food, would wander up to the farm, grandpa would let them bed down in the barn, and feed them for 3-4 days, then he would send them on their way with as much smoked mullet and biscuits as they could carry, my mama asked her daddy why he did that, and his reply was "be careful, you might be entertaining an angel", this Godly man lived by the scripture

Sometimes mama would get to have her cousins over to spend the night, boy that was fun, after dark they would get washed up, a pan of water was heated on top of the wood burning stove, and taken to the bedroom, I guess they all got bird baths, anyway it worked, well after they got cleaned up they would then go out to the north side of the house and lay on the grass for hours, then they would tiptoe back in and lay down on quilts on the floor, and softly giggle, they would stay up too late and wake up grumpy, but they sure had a good time doing it.

Once a month my mama got to go to town, her mother would get the mule hitched to the wagon, and they would head to Bonifay, they would go to the cloth store, grandma would buy a little cloth and thread, then they went to the general store, where they would stock up on flour and sugar, then sometimes my mama would get a 5C ice cream cone, boy she thought that was living "high on the hog", one day in town she saw a girl roller skating on the sidewalk and she was amazed.

My mama remembered the day that her brothers went "riding the rail "searching for work, they rode those train tracks, all the way to Kansas and found work, I can't imagine two boys hopping a trail like a couple of hobos, and sleeping in old boxcars filled with other men, men that were homeless, and hungry, but they made it, they worked for a year, and when they came home it was in a shiny automobile that they had purchased. But grandpa would have none of it, he wasn't impressed with that new -fangled auto, while the others were piling in that shiny red car, grandpa and granny they were hitching up the mule and riding to church just like always, I must of admit, I would of probably been one of the first's ones in the shiny red car. Changes came slowly for grandpa.

The floors had to be scrubbed on a regular basis, and there was a use for everything, after the wash was done on Monday, that hot soapy water didn't get wasted, no way, the floor was scrubbed with a corn husk broom, a scrub brush was made by taking a piece of cypress board, about 18 inches long and 12 inches wide, holes were drilled about every 2 inches and a dry corn shucks were forced into the holes, a long handle was put into the top, this corn shuck broom would really scrub the floors clean, but I now know what got the floor clean and shiny was the amount of elbow grease put on that mop handle.

A kitchen garden was planted every spring, they planted turnips-rutabagas-collards-tomatoes-cabbage-okra-onions-peas-butterbeans-sweet potatoes-Irish potatoes-pumpkins-cantaloupes and anything else that was edible.

Mama said that many of their goods from the garden were canned and put up for future meals, sweet potatoes were banked, this was a shallow hole dug and lined with pine straw, the potatoes were put in and covered up with more straw, a wooden cover was placed over the top, this kept the rain out, this way potatoes were kept over the winter time

The Irish potatoes were dug up and placed under the house to stay dry, they kept for a good long time that way, also the pumpkins were placed under the house to stay dry, cantaloupes had to be enjoyed right away, while they were fresh, peas and butterbeans were shelled and canned in glass jars, during the summer cabbage was cut up and packed in crocks to make sauerkraut, some of the corn was shelled and made into hominy.

I remember my daddy buying a block of ice from a man in town, he put it in a crocker sack…fancy name for a burlap bag, well our freezer on top of the fridge couldn't cool off butter and the freezer in the lean-to was filled to the rim, after he took an ice pick and chipped us all a little ice for our tea, I wondered how we could keep that block of ice from melting, and I asked him about it, he said just follow me, we walked around the house and under the magnolia tree he had dug a hole 2feet by 2 feet, they placed that burlap bag in the ground and covered it with straw and about 4 inches of top soil, and when we went back 3 days later to get more ice, it was still frozen, I asked how that t was possible, and my daddy explained that the underground was about 20 degrees cooler, and then my mama told me that was the same spot that her daddy buried ice, some 50 years earlier, I know one thing, those country folks seemed simple, but they could hack out a living on next to nothing and they ate like kings, it makes me proud that I'm just as tough as them and I got plenty of spunk and backbone to boot.,

After all of this was done, the yards had to be raked, and the leaves were placed in the cow pen

This made organic fertilizer for the next spring; of course back in the day it was just called compost. Early in the spring the dead foliage was burned off the fields, and then the ground and to be flat broke, plowing would start, the old plow was pulled by a great big old mule, he was 25 hands tall, and had an ornery disposition, I understand that my grandpa was a gentle man, but believe he wasn't afraid to let that whip crack if necessary, when all chances of a hard freeze were over then the ground was broken over and plowed up and then the planting would begin.

First the early crops were planted, tomatoes seeds were planted inside a seed box, and this was kept indoors because the young stalks were very tender, and they had to be cared for and nurtured so by the time it was warm enough to plant them outside they were fairly large plants, this made early tomatoes, early garden peas were put into the ground, and Irish potatoes were put in the ground, seed potatoes were always bought fresh and the eyes had to be cut out of the potatoes, the small piece of the potatoes that was left was boiled with dumplings In them, this was always a real good treat, by this time everyone was tired of canned or dried food, and to have fresh potatoes was a nice change.

Soon the coal burning trains and the horse and buggy were replaced with electric train engines and motor cars, electric lights then an electric pump and water pipes, what a glorious day, water piped into the kitchen, no more hauling water from the well in a heavy bucket,

During the summer they got to go to the creek, and I couldn't believe my ears when my mama told me about the outings of long ago, they all loaded up into two wagons, then they had a bumpy ,dusty hot ride to the creek, back then the women and girls swan together, and further down the creek, the men and boys swan, one man stood watch at the top of the hill and kept a watch over the women-folk, if a boy tried to sneak off with a girl, and they got caught, they practically got horse-whipped, there was no hanky- panky back then, and the women were covered from one end to the other.

Mama was in Bonifay high school when she met out father, for the 2nd time, they knew each other as children, our daddy was on leave from the navy and he asked grandpa carter if he could call on her, grandpa said...if she can stand it, then I can too...my daddy said his knees were knocking...thank God grandpa said yes, of course they fell in love and married 3 months later, and then produced a house full of youngens.

Grandpa and grandma continue to live on the farm, life went on day by day, year by year, the children grew up, John and Mable grew old, too old to farm anymore, and the farm was retired, the mule was sold and a much smaller one was bought to pull the buggy to church.

John and Mable were grandparents, the world was changing a new cycle of life had started, the more things changed, the more they remained the same, but I made my mama a promise that I would tell you children, and I have, these old family memories, have caused a stray tear to sting my eyes on more than one occasion, though my grandparents and parents are all gone , I take joy in their simple lives, I have inherited their uncanny ability to survive on next to nothing, I remember while raising you two boys, the many times I've hung on with a wish and a prayer, by the skin of my teeth, I shall survive all that is thrown my way, all of my kin are laying out back at new effort cemetery , so if you drive by on new effort church road, and blow the horn, don't be the least bit surprised, if you get a "Howdy" thrown back in you direction a floating across the wind.

My daddy's mama was Irene Andrews, I remember a pair of brown eyes and a great round body, she was surely a godly woman, and she never missed church, we lived in Bonifay and we didn't have a phone, well daddy said load up in the station wagon, I want to surprise my mama today, let me tell you when we pulled up, my daddy was the one that got the surprise, daddy said why ain't you in church, and my granny told us that the Lord told her", Irene, start cooking company is on the way", granny was sitting on the porch rocking, and she said come on in dinner is on the table we cleared that door, and I want you to know fried chicken, rice and gravy, greens and biscuits and cobbler sit on the table, and tea glasses were sitting there with ice in them and it wasn't even melted, my granny Andrews had an inside connection with the lord, and let me tell you the vittles were mighty fine. Granny is buried over in Callaway, and to this day she is surely missed.

I almost forgot, when I was 5 my daddy was shucking oysters, and I would run by and eat one, well I ate more than one, I still hold the record of most oysters eaten at once ,I ate 5 dozen and 2 oysters, I was 5 years old and nobody has ever came close to that record…bragging rights…

When we lost our beloved dog "trouble', my daddy wrote a poem about him, and my mama wrote a poem called 'the box", and I have included both to these, they sure are extra special to me, so sit back read my poems, and

Let a word or two soak in, I have done it, I have found the courage to share my written thoughts, poems, wishes and desires with the world, I hope that one word that you may read will change you way of thinking, or perhaps help you to realize that each person, man ,woman and child is unique, this has been a mission for me, and has given me much to contemplate besides cancer, and these writings are filled with love from my heart to you home...much love to all...Lisa Pelt....my email is lisa1959pelt@comcast.net...

ATTITUDE

Many times life
May seem unfair
Among burdens and strife
We surely have our share
Have you stopped to consider
Others that pass your way
Or are you too bitter?
To listen to what I say
Life is what you make it
You really must try
So for granted, don't take it
Not one extra day can you buy!

ANASTASIA

Let's go to Anastasia, I heard my mother say
We'll pick a day that's sunny, and find a nice place to stay
A journey we'll make together, so joyous and so carefree
We'll walk along the beach, and wet our toes in the sea
My mother missed this journey, we had so lightheartedly
    planned
She traveled a new destination, to stand on heavenly sand
I must go to Anastasia, my husband heard me say
We must travel there together, and not waste a single day
With miles to cross, and beaches to tread
With gusts of wind, and shifting sand
So our journey began, as John turned the car inland
And I caught a glimpse of the sea, a feeling g of absolute
    contentment
Washed completely over me, the sun was shining brightly
And warm upon our skin, I could hear mama singing
As the waves came crashing in, the crying of the gulls
Reminded me of the hour, our journey so complete
Filled us with such power, I'm so glad I listened to mama
And journeyed this destination, God, safely led us there
And met our every expectation, now I understand tender
    mercies
Even though mama is gone, God allowed her to journey with
    us
Then simply calls her home

A VESSELL

The body is a vessel
Surely mad of clay
And after many years
It simply crumbles away
When the soul departs
I know it is heaven bound
Waiting for that judgment day
When your deeds around you surround
Did you love your neighbor?
His trespasses to forgive
Or in your heart did hatred
Find a home in which to live
Will you stand with courage?
Proud of all you've done
Or will you seek to hide
From the mighty one
It's never too late
To change your ways
If only you would listen
Closely to what I say

BELOVED MELODY

I remember when we were all together, so long ago on that
  old farm
Flatbed trucks and a yellow school bus, and a pea patch from
  here to the barn
Dresses to make, and bread to bake, floors to scrub, and
  calluses to rub
Our cup runneth over from daylight to dawn
I now know the Lord gives strength to the weak
And courage to the meek, for our daily journey and beyond
Years have gone by, since mama and daddy have died
And to this day my heart still grieves
I feel a tear sting my eyes and I try not to cry; I now know
  "love Lifted Me'
I wish mama and daddy could hold my grandbabies, and gaze
  into their eyes of blue
And sing their "beloved melody", in voices so vibrant and
  true,
I strive to keep their memories alive, by stories I tell and
  photographs I share,
To their memories I shall remain true, returning to a world full
  of life
I thank God with all of my might, as I sing our beloved tune,
So close your eyes little darlings, and dream of a rainbow or
  two,
And if you should meet your great grandparents,
Remember they have always loved you…

BRIDE OF EDEN

The mansion stands deserted, the door requires no key
The family is no longer living, they have passed into eternity
A bride remains behind, Gazing out to sea
I caught a glimpse of white, I blinked my eyes
Her image was lost to me, she is gently beauty
White as a snowy dove, she really is truly
His one and only love, she wanders along the copula
In the pond her reflection I see, she waits for the return of her lover
From a battle, that he can't flee, the groom is dressed in confederate attire
In a uniform, threadbare and worn, the bride wears linen and lace
And a veil that is slightly torn, Separated by a force unseen
Stranded between two worlds I'm told, finally the two can exchange their vows
In a ceremony that will make them whole, Time held then captive
In the daylight hours they were kept apart, as the sun goes down they reunite
And become one heartbeat in the dark, in the fading of the sun
Between two streaks of light, a bride and groom embrace
And walk into the night…

CHEMOTHERAPY

Today was day 1, of a cycle of 3, chemo rushes through my
veins; I pray that it will sit me free

Free from this cancer which causes me pain, free from this
curse, which causes me shame

As this drug courses thru my veins, I feel the fire, I feel the
pain, and it takes away my very breath

And makes me wonder what will happen next, soon comes
pelvic radiation

One more hope, for my salvation, one more chance to fight
this fight,

Lord I pray the doctors have it right, late at night as everybody
sleeps

I pray dear God, my soul to keep, I simply ask for just one
more day

To spend with my loved ones, too many to name, the
grandbabies know I'll lose my hair

The funny thing is, they simply don't care, they love me the
same as every other day

Before my life cancer did invade, so when you see me without
my hair, know this I simply don't care

I care about my husband, grandchildren and sons; I know our
race has hardly just begun

We hold steadfast and stand on the word, knowing Jesus is our
heavenly Lord

Able to heal in a second's decision, or grant safe passage to a
heavenly destination

I will be here for as long as I can, and when I pass I will stand
on heavenly sand

Never shed a tear for me, I would rather you throw a kiss, I
    will catch it you see
And know this I will never be far away, which simply translates
    to love every day

Written 12 hours after round 1 of chemo 10/25/12 @ 02:30 am

CHILDREN

These small humans
Hearts made of gold
Boundless unending energy
Innocent carefree souls
They are in our hearts
Always on our minds
One day they shall depart
The apron string untwines
What lies ahead?
No man can say
We are not promised tomorrow
We are only promised today
Did I do my best?
I feel that I did
It is my greatest wish
To raise wonderful kids
When they leave the nest
And join the human race
I pray they do their best
Each and every day…

CODY AND TEDDY
(two loveable dogs)

Anita and Barry, our very dearest friends
Were so glad you crossed the ocean, and in Florida you did
    land
I know Cody and teddy were the best to be found, and in our
    hearts, joy does abound
Two loyal loving pups, with love they did surround
Now together they walk, they are heaven bound
Don't be surprised, if you should hear
A small bark in the night that will fill you with cheer
Or perhaps all is quiet, and you see the curtain quiver
Don't be alarmed, don't even shiver
It's just Cody and teddy watching from the side
For they know shortly, Lisa will be stopping by
For her weekly visit, or perhaps a chat
Or a spot of wine, and a chance to relax
Our two pups, we love them dearly
They are safely above, smiling so cheerily
Always remember the love that they gave
That love is more powerful, than any old grave
They watch even now, I know they are smiling
So lift you cup up and honor them proudly…

CHRISTMAS TIME

Christmas is a special time
Decorations abound
Tinsels, stars, pretty lights
All over our house and around
But it's more than pretty lights
As I sit around the table
I contemplate a child's birth
In a lowly stable
I'm sure it was very cold
As Mary endured her labor
She laid her first born son
In Bethlehem's manger
The North Star was very bright
Three wise men did see
They brought, gifts of gold, frankincense, myrrh
To lay at Jesus' feet
King herod wanted the child
As the wise men departed
They went the extra mile
The child they safeguarded
As, I decorate my Christmas tree
In colors of red and gold
I'm reminded of that first Christmas
So many years ago…

CONTEMPLATE

I see the flowers bloom
In the garden out back
I sit in my private room
I contemplate my accomplishments
Yes, I know there is good
And, I know there is bad
And, I know I should
Never, ever be sad
We have so much more
Than many others
We have hope and joy
To pass to each brother
So lift your eyes
And give thanks above
If only you would try
Others will return your love

DAD

If I could turn back the hands of time
I would surely try, I would turn them
So far back, that you would never die
All together, we laid you to rest
On that lonely day
Even though we were all together
The angels had taken you away
Though, memories still surround me
Many times when I sleep
I can see you, talk with you
Or, simply hear you speak
I can still hear your deep laughter
It filled my heart with joy
But now they're only tears
For the laughter, we can share no more
I guess what I'm trying to say
Daddy, you were the best
And I wish you were here today
Even though, in heaven, I know you rest

DEEDS

Many times I've been told
Life is what you make it
Power may make you bold
For granted don't take it
Power can be as bright
As the sun in its glorious zenith
Or as dark as a moonless night
With utter darkness it bringeth
Will you judge another, by your own deeds?
Or will you his trespasses forgive
We all have the right to be free
Just imagine you've completed the race
You have conquered all obstacles
You're in first place…

DRAGONFLY

My sisters shared a story
About a tiny little dragonfly
Her soul crossed the universe
For all eternity to fly
My mother believed in this story
With my sisters she did share
She said; "look for me in the morning"
A flutter of wings here and there
I thought mama had left us
Lost, alone and so forlorn
After we laid mama to rest
And said our final prayer
We were surrounded by dragonflies
They were simply everywhere
Now, I believe in their power
My heart simply sings
Mama dwells beside us
Guided by tiny wings…

DREAMCATCHER

Across the hill I see, where an Indian village lies
Women, men and children, from the pale face were forced to
    hide
They were here first, before the birth of our nation
Yes, they were made to depart, to an Indian reservation
Did anyone give them a choice? , I fear the Calvary bribed
Did anyone hear their voice, or see their courageous pride
I know they felt alone, many were sick and needy
To be taken from their home, for the sake of a peace treaty
If I had my choice, I would let them live
In the home of their birth, where two rivers run still
I would see the buffalo, standing tall and plenty
I would see the corn grow, the teepees would be many
I cannot change the past, even if I tried
Though I do not think, the past has truly died
We are all brothers, regardless of our skin
We are many colors; to god we are all kin
So as I watch an eagle soars, or sees a shooting star
I'm reminded of the Great Spirit's Voice
From his home so afar, it is my greatest wish
' That I call you friend, and for my ancestors deeds
I seek to make amends …

EASTER CELEBRATION

Long ago and far away, in a land across the sea
On a hill called Golgotha, Christ gave his life for you and me
The final hour drawing near, God's might plan at hand
Jesus' death signifies, eternal life for all man
They nailed him to a cross; they called him "king of the Jews'
Yes, he arose on Easter morn, the resurrection had came true
The stone was rolled from the tomb, Mary Madagalin found
    in dismay
For she feared they had taken, her beloved Christ away
Yes, she could clearly see him, as he arose in the sky
But, she couldn't touch him. for the ascension drew neigh
She ran to tell the others, sisters and brothers, that Christ arose
    that day
He died so that all men may be free, so listen to what I say
We have a choice to choose, one or the other,
Let's not let Christ's life be used in vain
Spread the good news, sisters and brothers
Christ lives in God's name…

FANTASY

A castle lies in ruins
Far across the sea
Twin torrents once stood in union
The past was destined to be
Far across the loch
Fields of heather abide
A banner of green plaid
A strength none can deny
A powerful war horse
A sword by his side
He led his clan by choice
His word they did abide
His bride was gentle beauty
Fair as a white dove
To him she was truly
His one and only love
Though the past is behind us
And the future we can't see
Memories linger thus
Were they real or fantasy?

HANDS OF TIME

I dream of a life with a mate
The substance fairytales are made from
A union between a woman and a man
Matched by a loving God
Two hearts beating as one
Two souls melting together
A union so very strong
Any storm, we will weather
Before the changing of the tides
Let me hold you close to me
The touch of your hand in mine
Fills me with intense peace
When our time on earth is done
We will hold our heads up with pride
And walk into the setting sun
Knowing the "Hands of Time"…

HUNTER'S LEGACY

Mom, do you remember the first moment you held me, and
gazed into my eyes of blue
Though we had first met, I hoped you guessed. I had always
loved you
Can you see Grey and me standing, side by side in the hall?
Surrounded by tennis rackets, tennis shoes, and bright green
tennis balls
Do you remember a small Scottish terrier, named simply
Angus Macfearson
I thought he was a boy, turned out to be a girl, yet the named
Angus was given
I know that you cried on our final goodbye, I can still feel our
fears, through the depth of our tears
But on that "Christmas eve', I was completely set free
Remember I no longer needed my earthly form, through my
final journey, hope was reborn
I conquered the grave through my final flight, now others can
live, laugh and love with all of their might
Our greatest creator in his infinite wisdom, gently reached
down in a moments decision
I now realize what truly is grace ; I have looked upon my
sweet saviors' face
He gently carried me in his loving arms, now I reside in my
heavenly form
I rest every day holding Angus Macfearson, we are never
alone, to my words please listen
Keep my memory alive, by photos and stories and precious
moments that will never die

Go ahead, laugh, dance, and make a wish to clear blue skies
And remember Hunter's legacy, and know I am close by

I LOVE YOU MOM ALWAYS
HUNTER

JOURNEY

As I walk this path
That many before me travel
I wonder of their journey
Of the dangers and the hazards
I know it's not easy
Sometimes we try to run
But, God gave us the victory
Through, Jesus Christ his son
Another wore the 'crown of thorns'
That dug so very deep
Another hung on the cross
Between two dying thieves
He made the sacrifice supreme
For our sins he died
Now he is our heavenly king
With him, we shall abide

LOST TREASURES

As I gaze across the waters
And wonder of its depth
I can clearly see the image
Of pirates and a ship
I think of those before me
That may have crossed this way
Did they safely reach the other side?
Or join a watery grave
I think I hear them calling
In voices so forlorn
Possibly warning of danger
Or inviting me to join their home
So, the treasures remain hidden
Riches jewels beneath the sea
Untouched by human hands
Was this justice or destiny?

MANDY THE SMALLEST FAIRY

All the fairies were called
To attend a special meeting
See, one small fairy was leaving the glen
And special gifts she would be needing
Hope arrived right on time
Followed by joy, through the door
And just around the corner was peace
And love was next for sure
Courage was there that day
She had lots of encouraging words to say
She gave strength when needed
She never had to be repeated
They sprinkled their gifts upon Mandy the smallest in the glen
To give her the strength to endure
Until she could return again
So fly little one, use your golden wings
Fly towards the setting sun, don't be afraid to sing
These gifts will carry our smallest fairy safely from the glen
And behold they are strong enough
To return her safely again

MELINDA

My great, great grandmother, Melinda, she arrived upon a ship
She was known as an immigrant, no English words passed
 her lips
She must have been frightened, as she crossed the might ocean
Though her home was in Scotland, to the Carolinas she would
 be going
Our customs must have seen strange, to a lass of 20
To herd cattle on the range, never before had she seen any?
I wander was she scared? as she traveled her new nation
I know she must have feared, grizzly's panthers and starvation
What made her leave her kin, far across the sea?
Some she never saw again, was it fate or destiny
Well I'm glad she had dreams of a brand new nation
She even met her husband on an Indian reservation
There love was very strong; they passed on to their children
Together they belonged, regardless of opposition
I know that there together, even upon this day
Many storms did they weather, never did they stray
No one should try to change, what is destined to be
Had they never met, surely I wouldn't be

MORNIN GLORY

The sky splits open
A bright light is seen
All of creation awakens
The birds begin to sing
The flowers stand so proudly
Their faces towards the sun
The birds lift up their wings
Their journey has begun
I break my fast with provision
Guided by hands unseen
Thanks for all you've given
My prayers, I begin to sing
The master of all creation
Cares for you and me
He walks beside us always
He is our heavenly king

NATURE

Some people fail to see
The beauty of a flower
But let nature be
I respect the power
Woods that are full
Of this animal or that
Darkness descends like a hood
Noises that growl and scratch
The owl is so solemn
On a limb he sits
He waits with patience enduring
For his prey he will surely get
Deer are in the woods
Many can't be seen
Wait, if you could
At night they will feed
Noises that go bump in the night
Can be pretty scary
I may run with fright
Please don't step on the berries

ONE CHILD

One child stood alone, in a world so cold
One child frightened, with nowhere else to go
Was this child guilty? of societies sins
Did he ever feel, that he truly had one friend
One child tried, to protect him that day
As others pushed and shoved, with a firm hand they moved
    away
Why, oh why is this world, Full of wrong and misdeeds
Prejudices blooms like flowers, hatred is the seed
That innocent life is over, simply gone away
All that remains is heartache, and memories that will fade
All of his hopes and dreams, Died with him that day
I wish I had known him, encouragement I could have gave
Who's to say what's right or wrong, or even what might have
    been
But if we could turn back time, that child would have many
    friends

PAIN

Woe there's suffering
When one lives with pain
Little to give
Much to blame
All the treasures
Many would exchange
To have good health
A fortune they would trade
One more chance
Is not to be
There is no defense
For this enemy disease
So live life to the fullest
Guard your health by watch
Don't let your defense be worthless
Seconds make minutes on a clock

POWER

Far across the sea, many years gone by
Castles, drawbridges, moats, swords crossed in the night
A brave and valiant lad, his armor made of silver
He was good not bad, he could abide no evil
A powerful warhorse, a falcon by his side
He led his clan by choice, they followed him with pride
His banner of purple, the color of heather
Would stand proudly, any storm they could weather
Should evil come to call, the swords would ring loudly
The evil would fall; the strong knight was lifted up proudly
Strength and courage are power, in the midst of evil and ruin
King Arthur's valiant knights, round a table having a reunion
Now all that remains is a castle, armor, swords upon a wall
But memories swirl around faster; I can hear the falcon call

RAINBOW

Does a man's color
Measure his worth
We should love each other
Regardless of our birth
There are many colors
In the rainbow to see
Red, green blue and yellow
Each one special to me
We are all unique
In our own way
Side by side we work
Side by side we should play
So remember this morning
As you start your day
God made us many colors
He has the final say

RECOLLECTION

When I was a child
On a country farm
We would ride a mile
And ride horses from the barn
We played into the night
Darkness would descend
But we felt no fright
For we were among kin
Down a long dirt road
A one room church stands
Many memories unfold
We met many a friend
Dinner on the grounds
Singing every Sunday
But chores did abound
Back to work on Monday
Those memories in my mind
So clearly I can see
The joy I can find
Reliving childhood dreams

SAFE HARBORS

I sailed across the horizon
A dolphin by my side
The sun was shining brightly
Seagulls were soaring by
I looked all around me
The water was my friend
The boat rose and fell
The waves came crashing in
As the horizon began to darken
Lightening filled the air
The tempest moved in quickly
I was seeking shelter to hide
So dark I lost my sighting
No land I could see
I prayed that God would spare me
As I asked on bended knee
I suddenly heard a singing
As my dolphin rose in the sky
His small eyes were gleaming
His smile so very wide
He led me to safe harbors
Suddenly he was gone
Yet, he awaits my next journey
As, I venture from my home

STRENGTH OF MEN

As I sail around the harbor, and glance across the bay
I see a towering oak tree, with moss that gently sways
I think of another era, days of long ago
Ladies in billowing gowns, carriages to ride to and fro
The sun shone so brightly, so warm upon their skin
They gazed up at their creator, happy to be among kin
As the hands of time move swiftly, much like shifting sand
Once they were here, now they are gone
Only headstones among the briars stand
I read the names quickly, searching for what? I'm not sure
Seeking to make a connection, between life and death, to
    secure
Yes, I want to see a spirit, perhaps even beside him stand
Then watch him cross over, as he stands on heavenly sand
Daddy and mama have left us, departed from this earthly form
Their souls reside in heaven, sitting beside a heavenly throne
They have glimpsed glory, and walked streets of gold
They sir with their heavenly creator, their journey complete
So I'm told

SUNSETS PAINTED GOLD

Look across the horizon
The Sunset gently fades, and washes the sky with colors
That signals the end of my day, a day that went so quickly
I didn't see it pass, Now, I'm left with memories
Some happy and some regrets, Life is but a journey, Love's a
    mystery
You hold it in your heart, with your hand you set it free
Lord, help me believe, my father once told me
About sunsets painted gold, a beauty sent from God above
To touch a human soul, others have passed before me
That walks this earthly way, Taking courage from each other
And sunsets that gently fade, Let us find common ground
Upon which we all may stand, and surely change our ways
To make us a better friend

TAPESTRY

If your life's deeds were upon a tapestry
Displayed upon a wall
What would others see?
When they come to call
Would they see happiness or Honor?
And above all peace
Or would they see misery
That loves company with no good deeds
Were your problems many?
Or very little cares
For your thoughts a penny
Did your burdens you share
I see a life of trying
As the story unfolds
No time can you be buying?
Be you friend or foe

TEMPEST

I gazed across the horizon
The waves crashed to and fro
The wind is screaming loudly
Sounds like a banshee to my soul
I shiver under the raindrops
Not sure of where to go
Seeking shelter from the tempest
The force of the mighty blow
I think about the pelicans
Praying that their okay
Did they seek shelter?
Or did the storm they brave
I escaped the tempest
The sun is shining brightly
My soul simply rejoices
My prayers were answered quietly.

TIME

Time waits for no one
So, I've been told
Each memory, I will treasure
And hold close to my soul
I think of the birth of my sons
Each birthday a celebration
Through torn jeans and skinned knees
My heart beats with jubilation
I think of the birth of my grandbabies
John and I are so blessed
We love being nana and poppy
And are better at it than the rest
When we close our eyes at night
And say our nightly prayers
We give thanks for much indeed
We know that the lord really cares

TIME TRAVEL

Shut inside, Windows open wide
I age 1000 years to your one
I know it's late, so don't hesitate
Our journey has just begun
Two souls that unite
One supporting the other
Searching for love
Longing for happiness
Surely we belong together
I will meet you between
Two rays of light
Simply known as night
The hours pass slowly
So don't fear tomorrow
Look only upward
Think upon these things
Our time together
Is a priceless treasure
Which makes us richer than kings?
Who's to say what might have been, what might be
As we travel, across the horizon
In the golden sunlight where we will spend eternity

TITANTIC

As I gaze across the waters
And wonder of its depth
I can clearly see the image
Of Titanic, the mighty ship
I think of its many passengers
That tried to cross this way
For the ones that safely made it
Many joined a watery grave
I think I hear them calling
In a voice so forlorn
Possibly warning of dangers
Or inviting me to join their home
I'm sorry jack didn't make it
His love for rose was strong
I'm glad she did him the honor
Of living and returning safely home
So the treasures remain hidden
Riches and jewels beneath the sea
Untouched by human hands
Was this justice of destiny?

WORK

Every day I rise
And go to a job
It's a wonder
A bank I haven't robbed
(Only joking Lord)
I buy my ticket
6 digits every week
I just can't pick it
My numbers you can keep
So back to the salt mine
No silver spoon in my mouth
My ancestors were kind
No money they left in the house
I guess they had it tough
Riding wagons and all
Those seats had to be rough
Hold on so you don't fall

MY CHILDHOOD

When I think of my childhood and I wonder way back
I can see that old house; some may call it a shack
I can see it all so clearly, in the closing of my eyes
Oak trees, magnolias, and palms, an old barn that reached the
    sky
Don't forget the flatbed trucks, or the trip to the creek
We waited all week long, to go and wet our feet
The cows didn't bother us, though they were there first
When we all came a running, those cows hit the dirt
There were pick nicks to pack, an old worn logging trail
The small ones played, the big ones worked like Heck
A turkey would chase you, an old tire swing
A mule my brothers would ride, a miracle their necks aren't
    broke
We hid mama's switches a lot; she started looking for lighter
    knots
Don't forget the outhouse, with panthers near by
You better run fast, unless you know how to fly
We spent a lot of time junking, all over this great land
Now I'm always stopping at somebody's garbage can
A pea patch from here to yonder, well brother it just didn't
    appear
We all had to work asunder; I assure you these calluses are
    real
The preacher came to dinner, the bullets hit the fire
He shouted "hallelujah sinner", we all ran a mile
The golden rule, we can recite, you can tell we turned out all
    right

All these memories make a family, one that held steadfast
 through the years
We are so grateful…Lord…for all we hold so dear

MY DREAM

I often dream
Of a place in the sky
That can't be seen
By the human eye
My dreams are beautiful
Although they are short
And are all in the country
Of a last resort
A place in the country
Upon a great hill
Away from the city
Where a river runs still
A place of no hurry
No work to be done
Just living and loving
And having great fun

MY DOLPHIN

Once again, I found myself, at the water's edge
Searching the horizon, looking for silver fins
The sun was shining brightly, and warm upon my skin
I heard the seagull's cries, the tide came rushing in
I could feel the excitement, Also anticipation
I wanted to see my dolphin, All week long I had been waiting
My eyes searched the water, As far as they could see
I scanned the entire surface, looking for only one thing
I glimpsed a silver streak, as he rose above the sea
He was neither shy nor meek, He sang loudly to me
One day I will join him, Out there in the waves
We will swim together, neither will be afraid
I believe in the power of nature, this creature is magical to me
To soar through the air, and swim for all eternity

MY FAMILY

Thinking about my father
This world he left behind
Thinking about his journey
To another place and time
Thinking about my mother
A heart that's made of gold
The way she loved her children
A beauty to behold
Thinking about my bothers
Leaves upon the tree
We shall live together
In perfect harmony
I'm gonna fly away
Just you wait and see
I'm gonna fly away
My spirit shall be free
When we cross that river
Jordan's stormy sea
We shall live together
For all eternity

ORANGE BLOSSOM SPECIAL

Daddy stood by the couch
Opened his pocket with a smile
Took out his old harmonica
Blew some tunes for a while
The sound of daddy's harmonica
Made my troubles seem to fade
Fed my soul completely
Always brightened my day
I wish for one more minute
I could hear it all again
Then get daddy a cup of coffee
And reminisce of all that's been
I loved to hear that old whistle blow
I swear that train was real
Coming faster and faster
Then simply to disappear
So in the dark of night
If you're lucky enough to hear
The sound of "Orange blossom special"
Remember…daddy is near

THE CALL OF THE WILD

Listen to the wind, a song it gently sings
Be you foe or friend, a message it will bring
In the deep of the woods, in an overgrown thicket
I see a newborn fawn, I hear the chirping crickets
Did you hear the call? , a lonely whiperawhirl
Did his mate fall? or is he merely filled with zeal
The panther hides at light, but at night he will prowl
Lock up the chickens tight; put the horses in the corral
Nature has many calls, sometimes it seems cruel
The weaker will always fall, the same for humans is true
We are all like these creatures, some can't be tamed
We need a strong teacher, or our minds will be lame
Search within yourself, don't think less of me
Let your fears depart, fulfill your destiny

THE CRYING OF THE GULL

I remember two young lovers
Who wrote their name in the sand?
Then walked into the Sunset
So content, hand in hand
The tide rushed in loudly
The sun started to fade
The gulls cried out proudly
So very small and so brave
I walked along the beach
The tide ebbed to and fro
The wind blew gently
I could feel sand between my toes
We each faced our destiny
So try not to be afraid
For when the gulls sing loudly
Have courage they simply say

THE EXTRA MILE

Would you walk an extra mile for your brothers?

Would you walk an extra mile for your friends?

Would you go through life, and do all the things

That it takes to be a woman or a man

THE FAIRY'S GIFTS

I saw a tiny fairy
She fluttered her tiny wings so
I thought of her heavenly gifts
She had the power to bestow
Her tiny face was gentle beauty
Quiet, serene, full of love
Her tiny delicate wings
Were as white as a snowy dove
She fluttered gently, ever so softly
Landing upon the ground
And I human saw her
Upon an earthly mound
I thought of the world
As, I made my fairy wish
Yes, she bestowed these gifts
With one little fairy kiss
No, I couldn't touch her
But, the gifts were received
I want to share with all mankind
Love, Hope, Joy and Peace

THE GARDEN

As, Jesus prayed in the garden
On that long ago night
I wonder of his burden
Did he perhaps feel any fright?
For the robe he wore
The soldiers tossed coins
His robe they exchanged
For a "Crown of Thorns"
He bore the cross with dignity
As he struggled uphill
But, his death gave us victory
Our sins he will forgive
The man named pilot
He helped destroy this man
Yet, he unwillingly helped
God, rule over our land

THE HEART

If, I look will I find love
Hidden in your heart
Or do you have dark secrets?
From which you can't part
If you walked in the light
Day, by day
Maybe, you just might
Listen, to what I say
If you extended your hand
And show love to your brother
Does that make you less a man?
Less than all the others
So, on your daily path
Guide your steps with love
Your troubles will be half
You're Soul, white as a Dove

THE HOMECOMING

Many, many years ago, our father we lost to horrors untold
The cancer that racked his body and mind, death brought relief
A flower was plucked from the vine, years later much to our
surprise
Our mother we lost, lord how I cried, our hearts were so heavy
Our pain we did bare, I foolishly wondered Lord, if you really
cared
As I laid me down for my nightly rest, I spoke my prayers, and
said "God bless"
The most wonderful dream appeared before my eyes, I was
standing in the kitchen
Mama and daddy were by my side, there stood daddy with a
harmonica in his hand
Wearing checkered Bermuda shorts, a tank top, and flip flops
full of sand
Mama's pretty red hair, was curled upon her head, her smile
was so beautiful, her lips were ruby red
I blinked my eyes and looked at my mother, the door opened
wide, in walked sisters and brothers
As Mama and daddy got to meet the great-grand's their eyes
were full of love
There they stood side by side, holding hands
The coffee cups were lifted; the food we did share, the room
was full of magic and cheer
The sands of time pass slowly, one grain at a time, Lord; I'm
reminded of your "Tender Mercies"
As you nurture the remaining flowers on the vine

THE LOGGING TRAIL

Across yonder highway, lies an old worn logging trail
Twisting, turning, and spiraling, covered with palmetto and
    split pine rail
They left before daybreak, my father and my brothers
They had their quota to make; they worked hard to help each
    other
They drove down a dusty dirt road, to toil in the blazing sun
They worked hard to make a whole load, so they could make
    a run
He saw had to be sharpened; the old truck sprang a leak
Mama prayed for rain, daddy prayed for relief
We brought beans and cornbread, mason jars filled with ice
    tea
Lord, I swear we were starving, mama prayed before we could
    eat
My hands were covered with turpentine, they stuck to one
    another
Had to cut it with kerosene, the smell was, well Oh brother!
I love the sound of timber, as it hits the ground
I can feel the earth tremble, limbs around me surround
Blood, sweat and tears, all ran together
Made us all so strong, any storm we can weather
Well daddy didn't complain none, those calluses were many
From daylight to dark, the workload was plenty
Many times after our cutting, we headed to the creek
To wash off all of our labors, and simply find relief
Though my childhood is over, my memories are my own
I can feel a mighty hand, safely lead me home

I can see that old worn logging trail; I can still smell fresh cut
   timber
Surrounded by a golden sunset, my creator, I will remember

THE LONELY CASTLE

There is a coat of honor
Displayed upon w wall
Of a once mighty fortress
With twin turrets so very tall
Surrounded by a moat
With a drawbridge and Iron Gate
Be you friend or for
Whoa if your one to hate
Twin thrones upon the dais
Fit for a king and his queen
Knights with their shiny armor
Protect all to be seen
Knights upon a white charger
A mighty and fierce war horse
His hooves could be as deadly
As the gauntlet or the sword
That way of life is over all that remains is antiques
No more to sit upon a throne
And pass judgment upon the meek

THE LONG JOURNEY HOME

Concetta, I love you said Giuseppe, as he gently held her hand
I promise you a new life, in a great new land
In a land called America, A man can be free
To work so very hard, and meet his every need
Though he journeyed alone, and left Italy behind
Concetta and the children, Were always on his mind
Though the ship was crowded, and the fare was meager
When he saw Paris island, His heartbeat on so eager
Soon his family joins him, proud to be by his side
Another generation arrives. Fills him with so much pride
The young man named tony, with eyes so very brown
Fall in love with Miss Libba, joy around his heart surrounds
They are blessed with two young sons, they journey this great
      nation
They make their home in Abbeville, filled with love and
      jubilation
Now the sons are grown, working to make a living
Great southern wood is born; I call it pine tree preservation
The hands of time move swiftly, so many years from the start
This humble family has succeeded, and remains so very dear
      to our hearts

THE PIRATE

Through the fog I see, many sails that billow
A mast as big as a tree, I hide my head on the pillow
This ship that sails at night, seeking only treasure
Yet, I fear the captain, is surely seeking pleasure
Pirates, outlaws, heathens, many names of dread
Guard your life without hesitation, or you will end up dead
Hide your gold and silver, hide yourself as well
Fear will make you shiver, go and ring the church bell
If we all stand together, surely we won't fall
We will fight the enemy, we will protect our hall
So hide your treasures, run for your life
The pirate seeks pleasure, among the pain and strife
Flee up the hill, there stands a cave
Be quiet and very still, or your life you might trade.

THE SENTINEL

I gaze across the grounds, a majestic oak I see
His outstretched branches abound, Seem to reach to eternity
This mighty tree watched the Indians, So very courageous and
    strong
Until the white's man treaty, Forced them from their home
This oak has seen covered wagons, Filled with families from
    different nations
Seeking a new life, in a new land, faced with grizzly's panthers
    and starvation
This tree watched a young nation that hatred tore asunder
With colors of blue and gray, and cannons that roared like
    thunder
I wonder could he hear the voices, of others that passed this
    way
Seeking shelter under his branches, at the closing of their day
I stand amazed in the presence, of such infinite grandeur
The moss gently swaying, my journey home I have secured
Underneath his branches, his voice touches my very soul
Filling me with inspiration, strength for my journey, as I go
The lone sentinel, 600 years strong
Has withstood the test of time, so tall and so alone
His Love for mankind, so divine

THE SHEPARD

I see a tiny sparrow
I'm reminded of the power
I think of our creator
He watches every hour
Though our thoughts are our own
The path we travel is narrow
It is so very easy to fall
I think of that one small sparrow
If I had the faith
Of one grain of mustard seed
There would be no hate
There would be no enemy
Many sheep will fall
Along the rocky path
Many will stumble and fall
They keep looking back
Don't feel that you're alone
There is one that guides
He will lead you home
With him you will abide

THE SLAVE

I once heard a story told, from a long time ago
That pieces of 8 were traded, for a man's very soul
Men, women and children, stolen in the dark of night
Forces on a slave traders ship, regardless of their fright
Their journey out of Africa, must have been a living hell
Many died along the way, a watery grave awaited them there
Never to see their kin again, or know their mothers love
Forced to stand on the auctioneer's block, I know they shed
     tears and blood
What gives a man the right, to measure a man's worth
Based upon the color of his skin, given to him at his birth
Hatred was the sickness, prejudice was the disease
I often wonder Lord, how could this ever be?
I cannot change the past, even if I tried
But, I can stand tall, and guard each man's pride
And live by the good book, and let it my conscious guide
The great emancipation, thank God, changed our land
Lord, help us to reunite, and spread your word to all men
America is a great nation, let the whole world see
Our strength binds us together, thank you Lord, we are all free

THE TRUNK

I found an old trunk
That was left alone the way
I wandered of its journey
Treasures that another saved
I thought about its contents
Buried oh so deep
I knew I had to open it
If only for just one peek
So, I opened up the top
And much to my dismay
The trunk was mostly empty
Only several things remained
Three neatly folded kerchiefs
One old tarnished Tierra
Pieces of quilting scraps
And one gray feather
So, I gathered up my treasures
And went alone my way
Now they reside in my attic
Just in case of a rainy day

THE VIKING

Many, many years ago
From a land called Iceland
Came warriors with eyes of blue
Simply known as Vikings
A large wood hulking vessel
With many men aboard
They were surely seeking treasures
Silver and gold they would hoard
They would move a castle
One rock at a time
They kept coming faster and faster
I can see them in my mind
Once they were on land
A powerful force to behold
They held together like a clan
They would steal your very soul
So hide your treasures
Run for your life
The Vikings seeks pleasure
Among the pain and strife
Flee up the hill
Enter the dark cave
Be quiet and very still
Or else you life you may trade

Anastasia ... regards a trip planned but the actual route and time changed by circumstances

Bride of Eden ... bride and groom lost in time

Dad ... loss of my Father

Dragonfly .. loss of my mother

Dream catcher ... the plight of the American Indian

Melinda ... my grandmother that came from Ireland

My Dream ... the first poem I ever wrote

My dolphin ... just sharing my love of Dolphins

One child ... the loss of one child in a cold world

Pain ... my father's battle with cancer

The slave ... tells of the horrors endured, because of the color of one's skin

The sentinel... I tried to be the voice of a 600 yr old Oak Tree

Through my Fathers eyes ... Mans journey to the Hereafter

There are many more and I hope that you will read them all, it has always been my desire, to share my gift, whether in written or spoken word, or song, I seek to make the world a better place.

LISA ANDREWS PELT

When we lost our beloved Dog "Trouble" we were heartbroken, Daddy was able to catch a wide range of emotion when he recited "Trouble", and when my Mother recited "The box" I was filled with excitement, I have committed these to memory,(the emotions that I felt), and many, years later they still bring me joy. I hope that you have read one word, that has perhaps given you hope, courage, or perhaps just brightened your way, or just plain and simply renewed your faith, we are never truly alone, and each day is a gift.

"TROUBLE"

Our Father's
Tribute to
Our Coon Hound
Trouble

Well, here lies old trouble,
he's finally gone to rest,
he'll never be forgotten, I Rated
him As the best,
we hunted wild hawgs together,
& i think he would have fought A ber
there was never A better mix bree
cur, no other could compare,
oneday we were going hunting
& we're walking A woodside trail,
when old trouble snatched A Rattler
from under my feet, As far de as An
old fence Rail, they fought A fierc
battle, & I seen Right off he'd won,
that old cur dog & friend of mine,
was A fighting son of A cur.
my Heart is saddened by his
leaving, but yet is Gladdened Again,
cause he had grown old & weary
& was sick & full of pain.
one day not long before his time,
his sight had grown very dim,
he pulled Another snake from
near my feet, this time twas
A fallen tree limb.
it didn't seem to shame him though
when he seen what he had done,
he just Run in circles & barked &
grinned, that lovABle son of A cur.
So friend if you've ever out

Father

So stop + pause for a moment
+ hold you're hat in you've hand
for below you lies buried,
where in my ARMS i carried, Not A dog
but A couvageous old man.

83

TROUBLE

(Our Father's tribute to our hound)

Well here lies old trouble, he's finally gone to rest
He'll never be forgotten, I rated him as the best
We've hunted wild hawgs together
And I think he would have fought a bear
There never was a better mix breed cur
No other can compare, one day we were going hunting
And were walking a Woodside trail
When old trouble snatched a rattler
From under my feet, as large as a fence rail
They fought a fierce battle, I'd seen right off he'd won
That old cur dog and friend of mine, Was a fighting son of a
     gun
My heart is saddened by his leaving, but yet is gladdened again
Cause he has grown old & weary & was sick & full of pain
One day not long before his time, his sight had grown very
     dim
He pulled another snake from near my feet, this time was a
     fallen tree limb
It didn't seem to shame him though, when he'd seen what he'd
     had done
He just ran in circles and barked and grinned, that lovable son
     of a gun,
So friend if you're ever out here, Stop and pause for a moment
And hold your hat in your hand, for below you lies buried,
Where in my arms I carried, not a dog, but a courageous old
     man.

Children

This is a very special box
It's full of many things
There's lot of real good memories
And lot's of hopeful dreams
Look at all the things you've done
Count them one by one
And when this day is over
You've hardly just begun
There are gymnastic tights
And pillow fights
And Barbie dolls to hold
And all the things you want to do
When you get big and bold
It's full of bees and butterflies
And rainbows full of gold
There are hummingbirds and raindrops
And Sunsets to behold
This is a magic box, you see
It's full of many dreams
There are caps and gowns, and wedding rings
And lots of other things
Just open up this magic box
And one thing you will see

It's always very full of love
From Grandpa and from me
Here is the afghan that I've made
It's really very small

The little thing won't cover you up you're really much too tall
I'll make more squares for you
I'll make them one by one
I'll keep adding them to it
Until the whole things done
I promised you an afghan
I didn't say just when
I'll probably have it finished
By the year 2010.

EXUM ELLIOTT

Exum Elliott was born August 28, 1825. He died on July 23, 1892.

This is an excerpt from the book, "History of Grant County".

In 1875 Mr. Carey* was married in Back Creek Church to Miss Ruth T. Elliott who was born i Miami County, Indiana on November 6, 1855, but when nine years of age she came with her parents t Grant County, where they located in Mill Township. She is a daughter of Exum and Hulda (Knigh Elliott, both natives of Grant County and successful farmers of both Grant and Miami Counties. The died in this country in advanced life. Mrs. Carey is a woman of exceptional character and qualities Since she was eighteen years of age she has been a minister of the Friends Church, preaching in th Back Creek and in the Friends Church at North Grove, Indiana. She has preached at many othe places and occasions, and is known as one of the ablest exhorters to be found among ministers of th church body. Her work has reflected forth many excellent qualities that are inherent within her, an few have wielded a greater influence for good than has Mrs. Carey wherever she has gone.

Mr. John T. & Mrs. Ruth T. (Elliott) Carey

Four children came to brighten the home of Mr. and Mrs. Carey; Maud, the first born, died is infancy Ida, the second, died at the age of eighteen years. Gervas Albert Carey has been a pastor and ministe in Friends Church since twenty years of age, but is now a student and teacher in Friends' University Wichita, Kansas. His wife was formerly Amy Gitchel. They have two daughters, Ruth and Elizabeth. The youngest child, John Stanley Carey, is engaged in operating his father's farm and has demonstrate his capacity as an agricultural man and in no uncertain terms. He has given special attention to stocl raising and his success has been praiseworthy. He married Callie Leota Thomas and they have on daughter, Pauline Louise.

Would you like to see your manuscript become a book?

If you are interested in becoming a PublishAmerica author, please submit your manuscript for possible publication to us at:

acquisitions@publishamerica.com

You may also mail in your manuscript to:

**PublishAmerica
PO Box 151
Frederick, MD 21705**

We also offer free graphics for Children's Picture Books!

---

www.publishamerica.com

CPSIA information can be obtained at www.ICGtesting.com
Printed in the USA
LVOW130903270313

326202LV00001B/2/P